2ND EDITION

Love Songs of the '50s

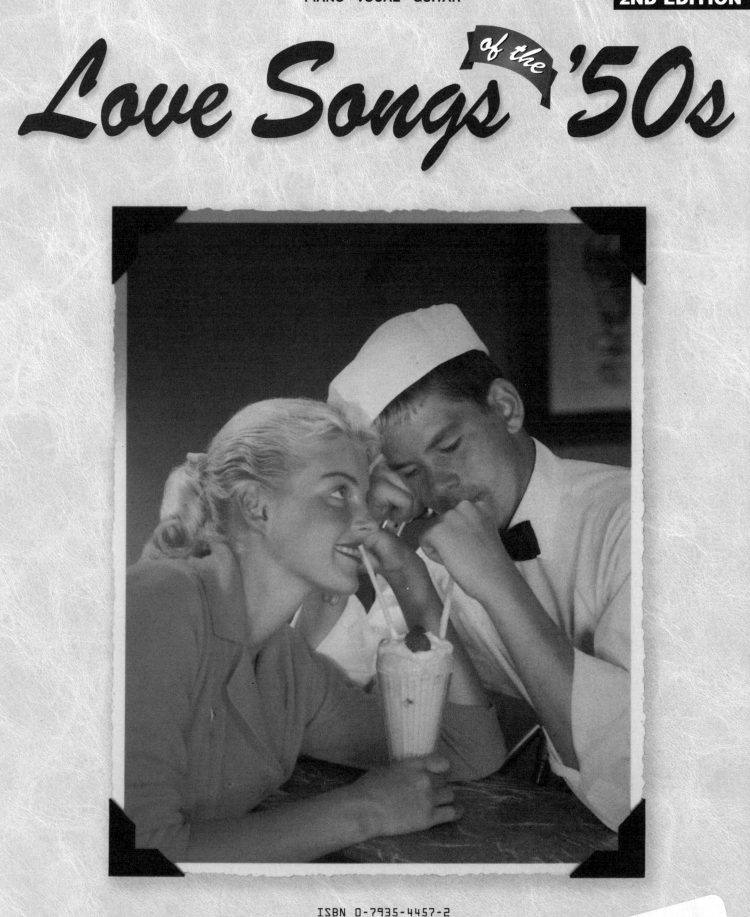

ISBN 0-7935-4457-2

HAL•LEONARD®
CORPORATION

7777 W. BLUEMOUND RD. P.O. BOX 13819 MILWAUKEE, WI 53213

Visit Hal Leonard Online at
www.halleonard.com

Contents

ALL I HAVE TO DO IS DREAM

Words and Music by
BOUDLEAUX BRYANT

Moderately

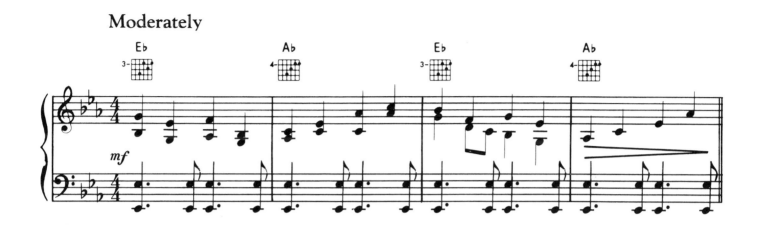

Dream, _____ dream, dream, dream, _____ dream, _____ dream, dream, dream. _____ When

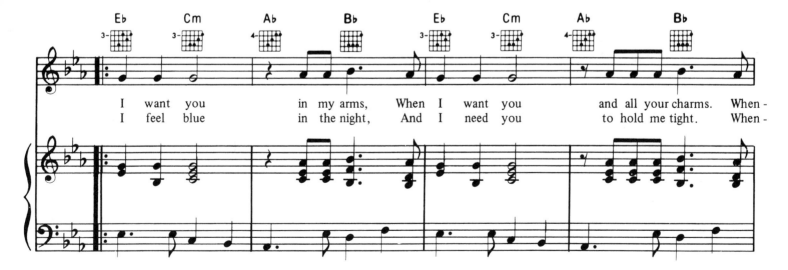

I want you in my arms, When I want you and all your charms. When

I feel blue in the night, And I need you to hold me tight. When-

ev - er I want you ___ all I have to do is dream, ___

ev - er I want you ___ all I have to do is

dream, dream, dream. When dream. ___

I can make you mine, taste your lips of wine, an - y - time, night or day.

On - ly trou - ble is, Gee whiz, I'm dream - ing my life ___ a -

ALL AT ONCE YOU LOVE HER

from PIPE DREAM

Lyrics by OSCAR HAMMERSTEIN II
Music by RICHARD RODGERS

The ro- mance that you have wait- ed for will come when it comes, With-

out a word of warn- ing it will start. With a

sud- den blare of trum- pets and the rat- tle of drums ___ A

dream will take pos-ses-sion of your heart.

Refrain (*slowly, with expression*)

You start to light her cig-ar-ette And all at once you love her. You've scarce-ly talked,

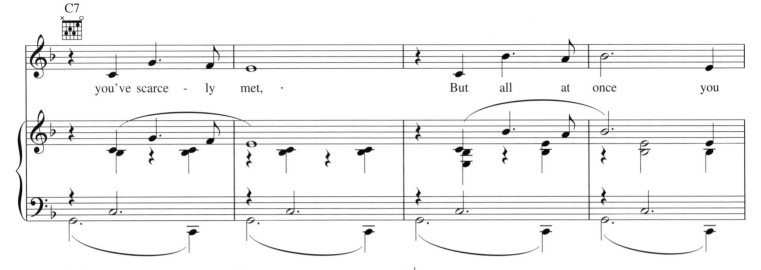

you've scarce - ly met, But all at once you

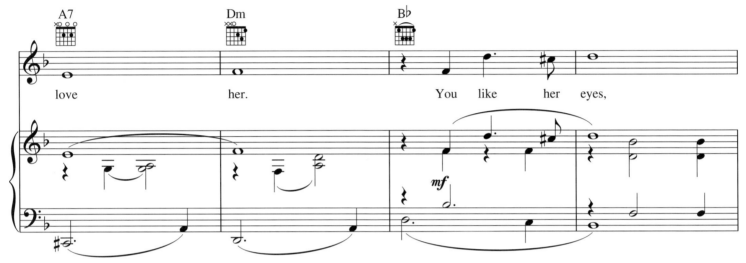

love her. You like her eyes, You tell her so. She thinks you're wise and

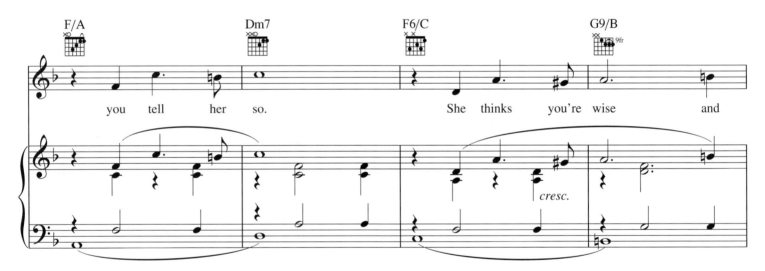

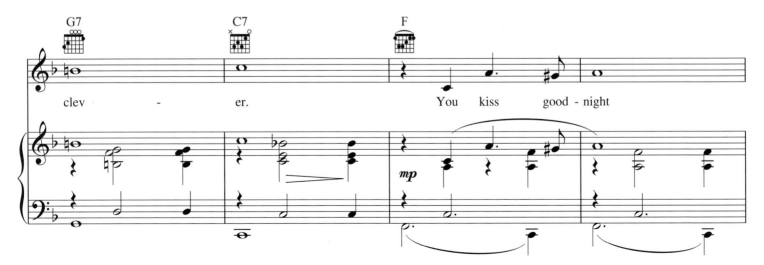

clev - er. You kiss good - night

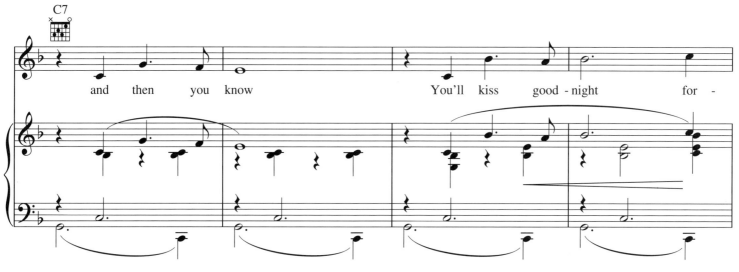

and then you know   You'll kiss good-night for-

ev - er.   You won - der where

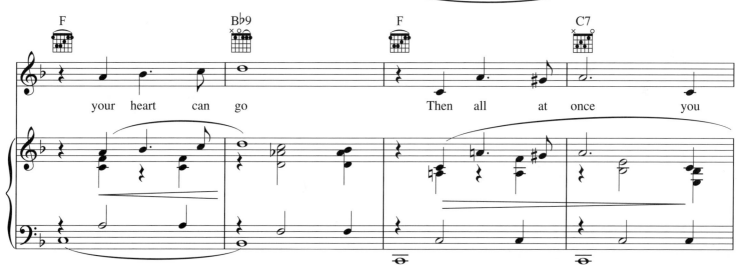

your heart can go   Then all at once you

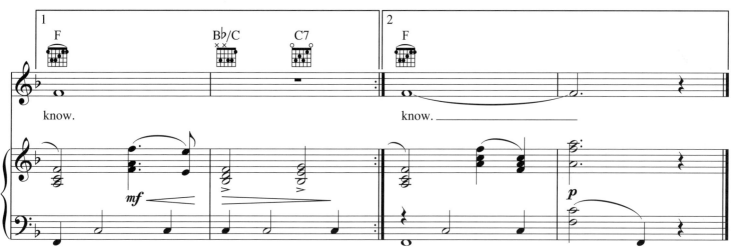

know.   know.

AUTUMN LEAVES

English lyric by JOHNNY MERCER
French lyric by JACQUES PREVERT
Music by JOSEPH KOSMA

Slowly, with much feeling

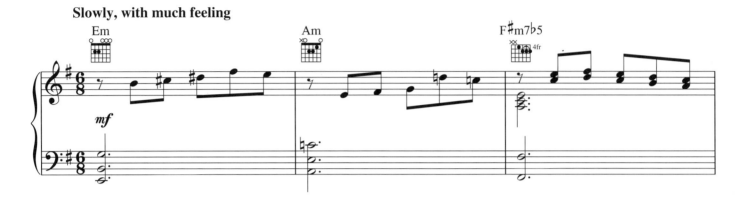

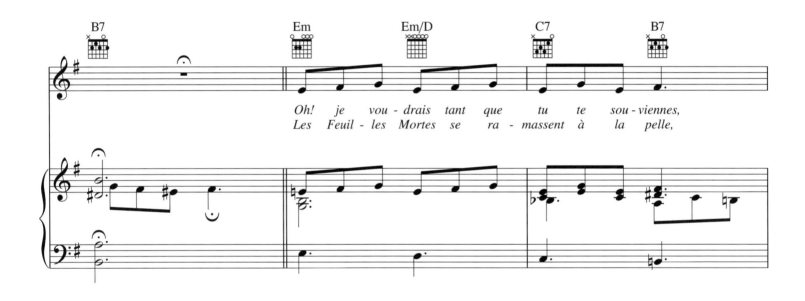

Oh! je vou - drais tant que tu te sou - viennes,
Les Feuil - les Mortes se ra - massent à la pelle,

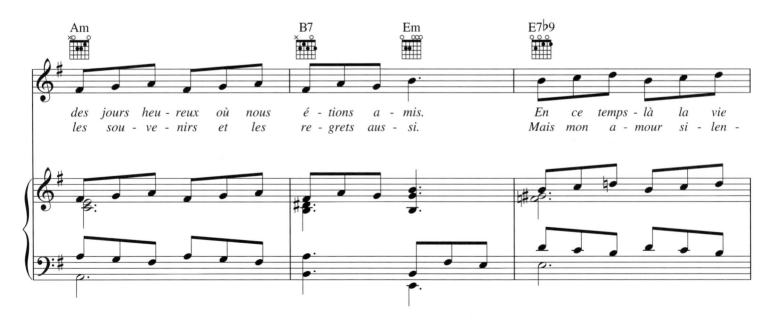

des jours heu - reux où nous é - tions a - mis.
les sou - ve - nirs et les re - grets aus - si.

En ce temps - là la vie
Mais mon a - mour si - len -

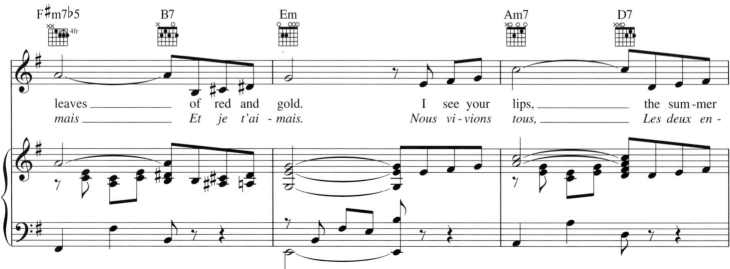

15

CHANCES ARE

Words by AL STILLMAN
Music by ROBERT ALLEN

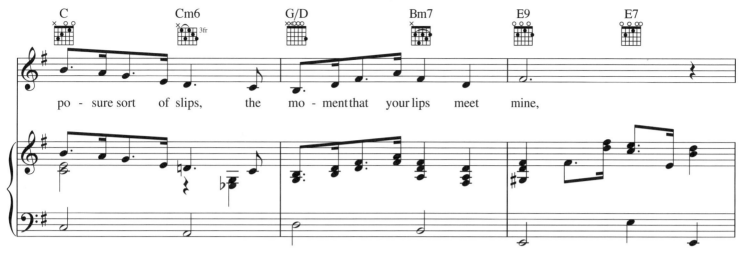

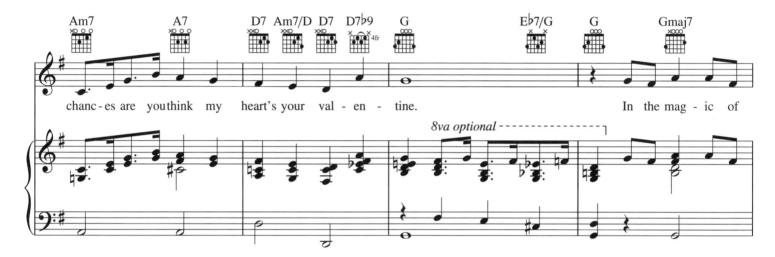

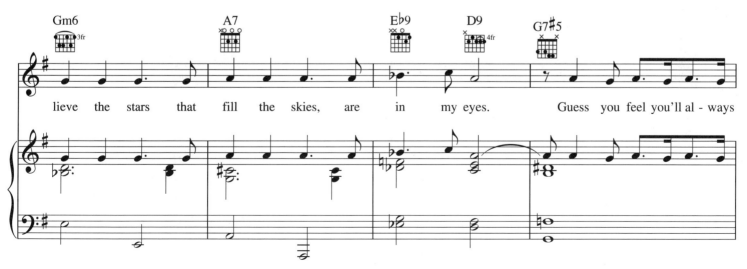

DO I LOVE YOU BECAUSE YOU'RE BEAUTIFUL?

from CINDERELLA

Lyrics by OSCAR HAMMERSTEIN II
Music by RICHARD RODGERS

Moderato

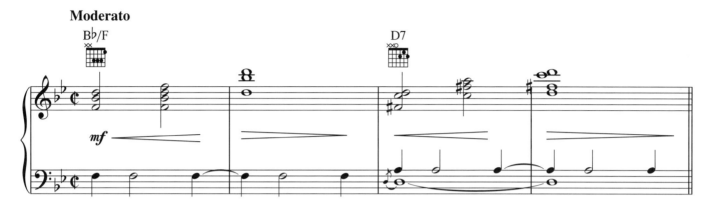

Refrain (*slowly, with warm expression*)

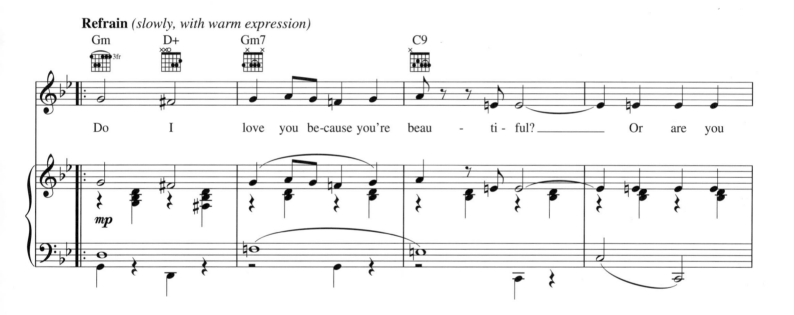

Do I love you be-cause you're beau - ti - ful? _____ Or are you

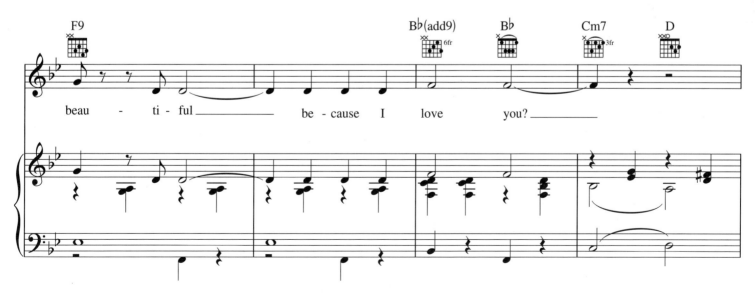

beau - ti - ful _____ be - cause I love you? _____

ENDLESSLY

Words and Music by CLYDE OTIS
and BROOK BENTON

Brightly

High - er than the high - est moun - tain _____ and deep - er than the deep - est sea, _____

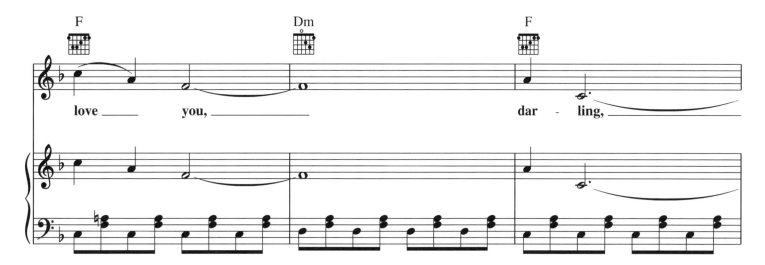

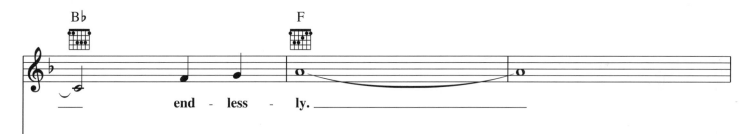

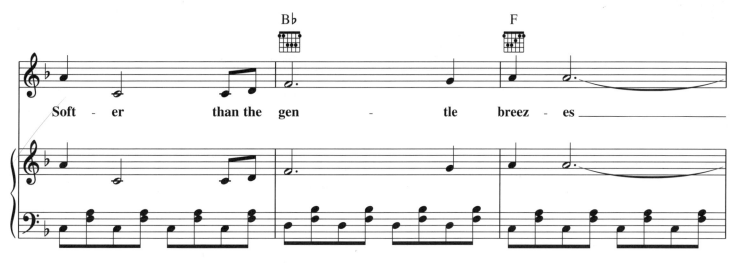

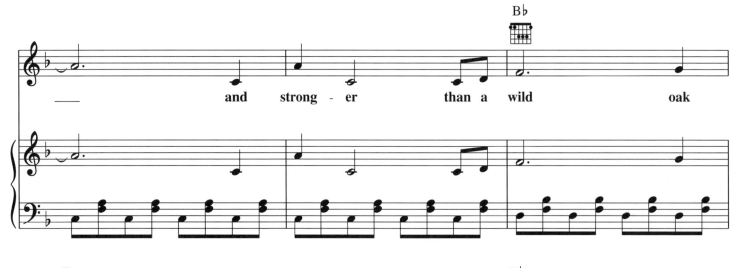

and strong - er than a wild oak

tree. _____ That's how

I will hold ____ you, _____

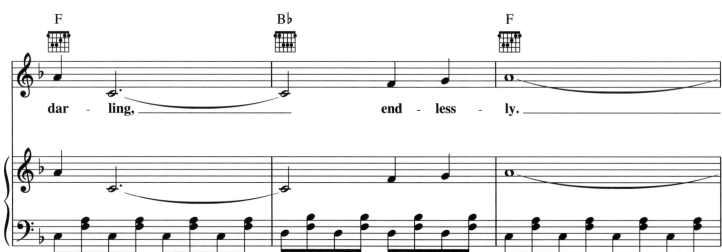

dar - ling, _____ end - less - ly. _____

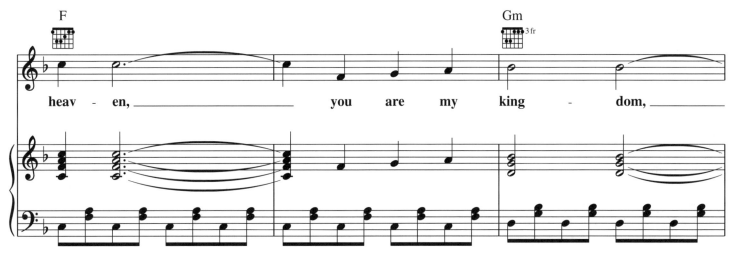

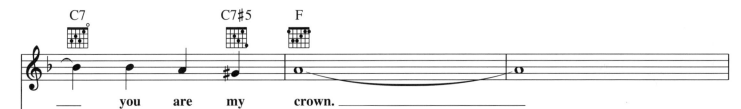

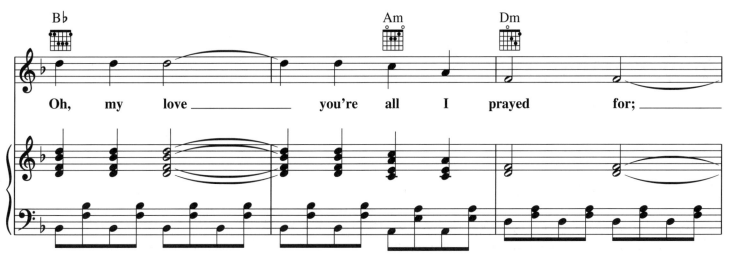

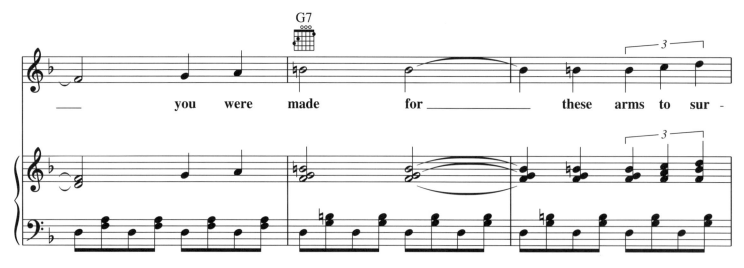

you were made for _____ these arms to sur -

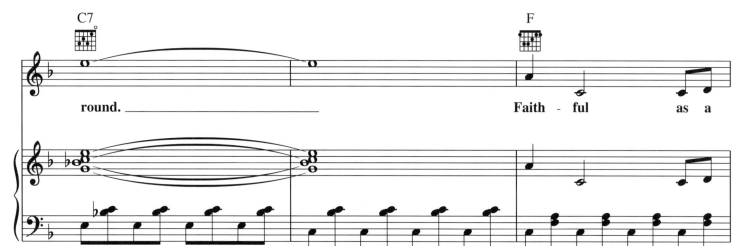

round. _____ Faith - ful as a

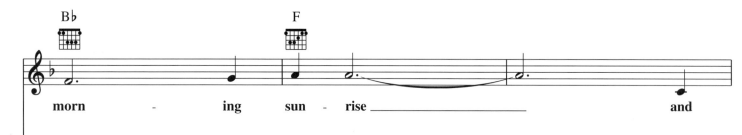

morn - ing sun - rise _____ and

sa - cred as a love can be, _____

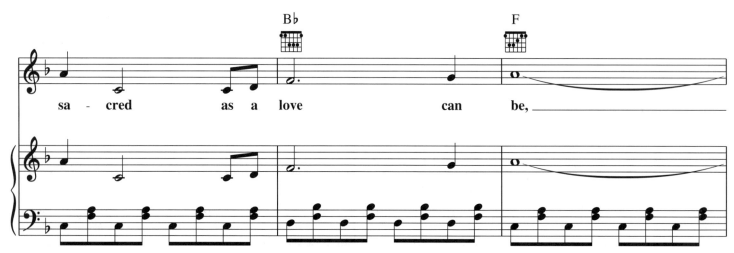

FLY ME TO THE MOON
(In Other Words)
featured in the Motion Picture ONCE AROUND

Words and Music by
BART HOWARD

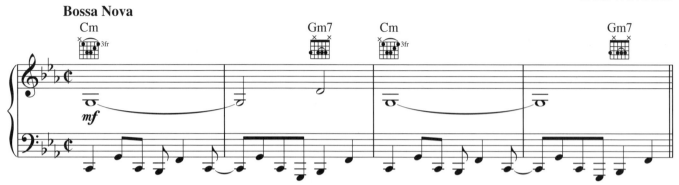

Fly me to the moon, ___ and let me play a - mong the stars; ___

Let me see what spring ___ is like on

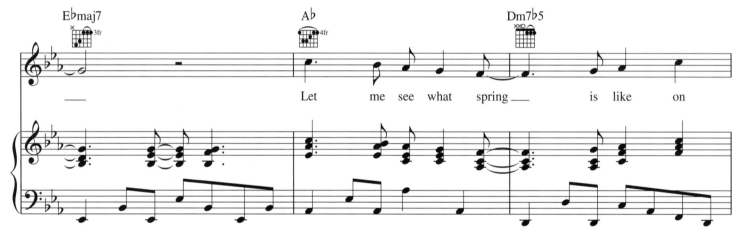

Ju - pi - ter and Mars. ___ In oth - er words, ___

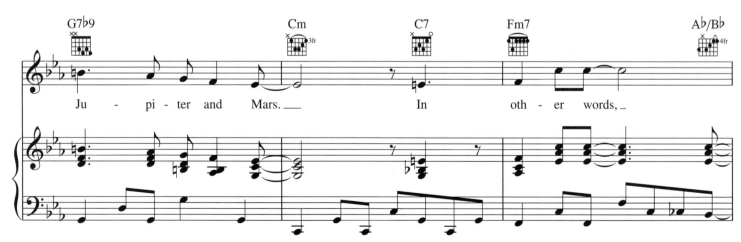

hold __ my hand! _____ In

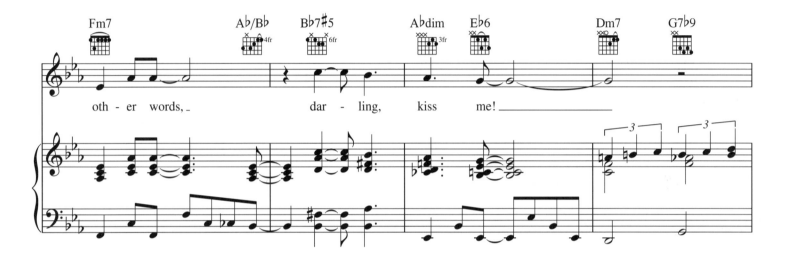

oth - er words, __ dar - ling, kiss me! _____

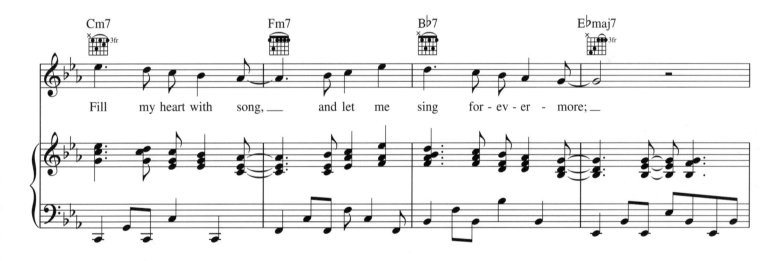

Fill my heart with song, __ and let me sing for - ev - er - more; __

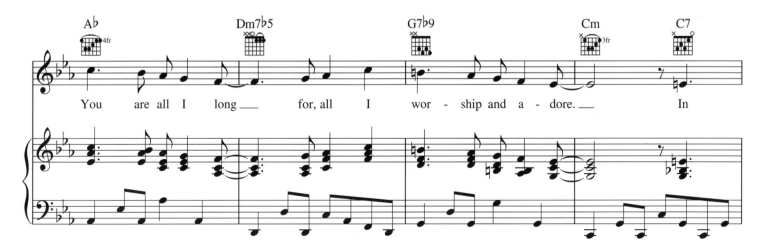

You are all I long __ for, all I wor - ship and a - dore. __ In

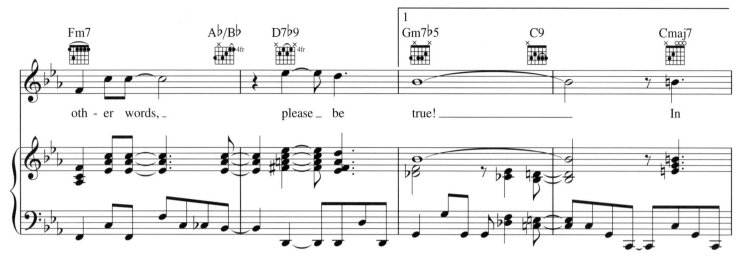

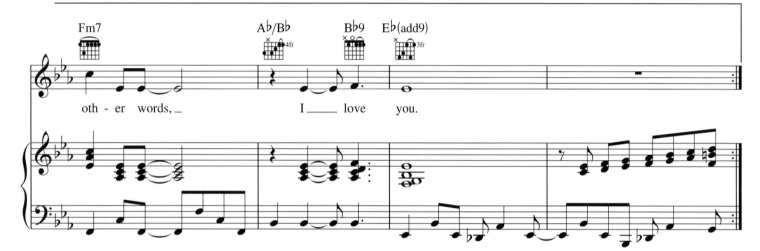

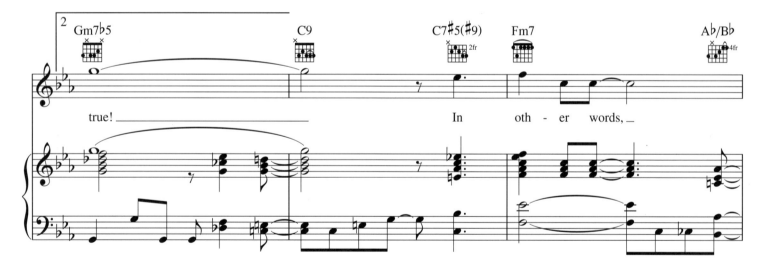

GOODNIGHT MY LOVE, PLEASANT DREAMS

Words and Music by GEORGE MOTOLA
and JOHN MARASCALCO

Lyrics:
Good-night my love, pleas-ant dreams and sleep tight, my love.

May to-mor-row be sun-ny and bright and bring you clos-er to me.

Be-fore you go,

HELLO, YOUNG LOVERS

from THE KING AND I

Lyrics by OSCAR HAMMERSTEIN II
Music by RICHARD RODGERS

Molto Moderato

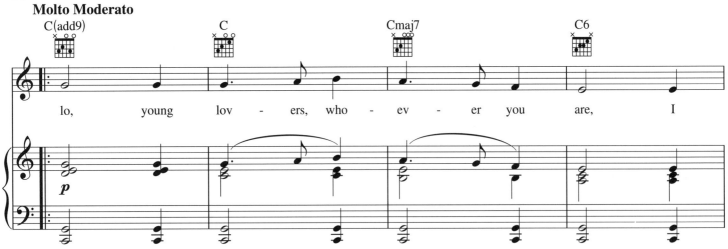

lo, young lov - ers, who - ev - er you are, I

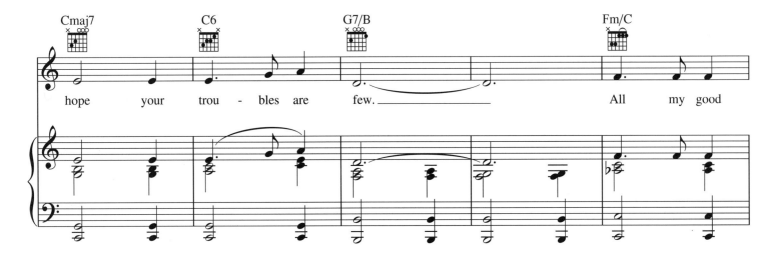

hope your trou - bles are few. _____ All my good

wish - es go with you to - night, I've been in love like

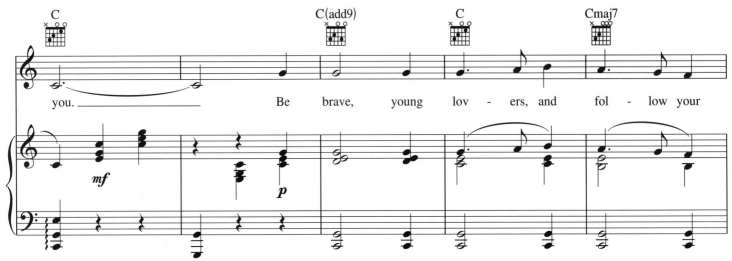

you. _____ Be brave, young lov - ers, and fol - low your

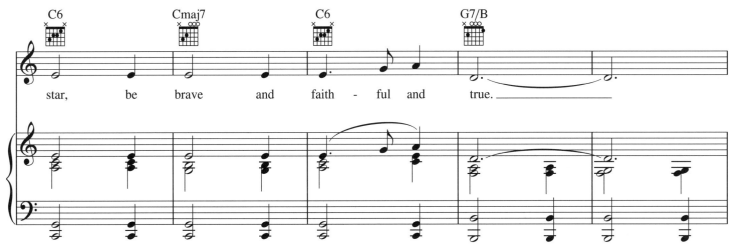

star, be brave and faith - ful and true. _____

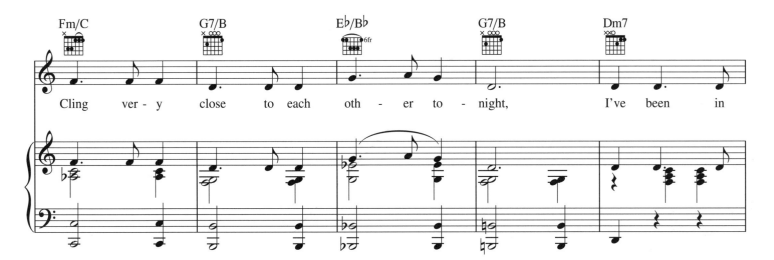

Cling ver - y close to each oth - er to - night, I've been in

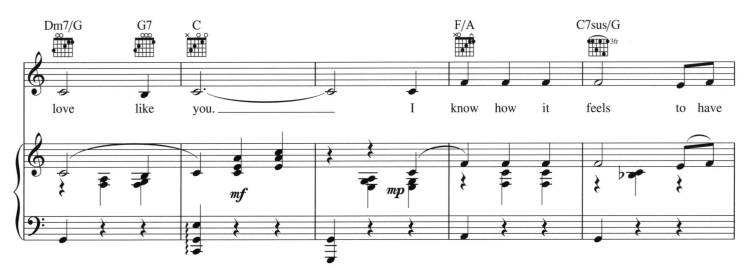

love like you. _____ I know how it feels to have

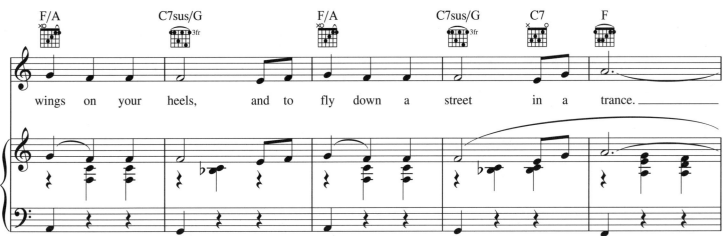

wings on your heels, and to fly down a street in a trance. _____

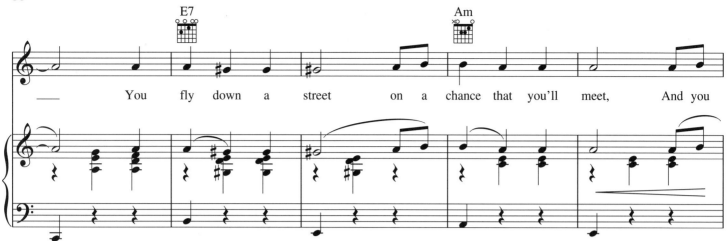

You fly down a street on a chance that you'll meet, And you

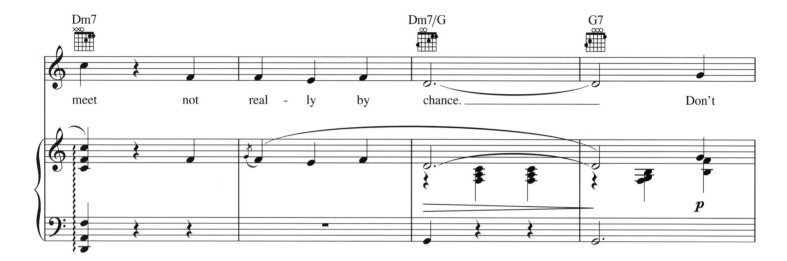

meet not real-ly by chance. _____ Don't

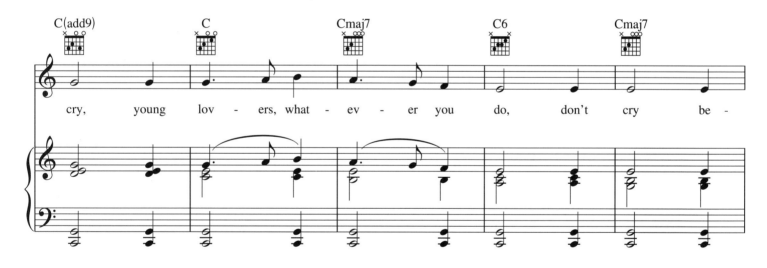

cry, young lov-ers, what-ev-er you do, don't cry be-

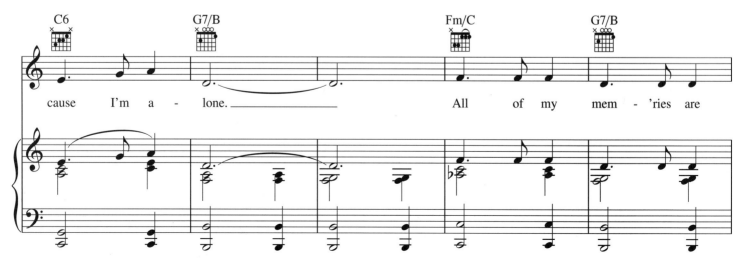

cause I'm a-lone. _____ All of my mem-'ries are

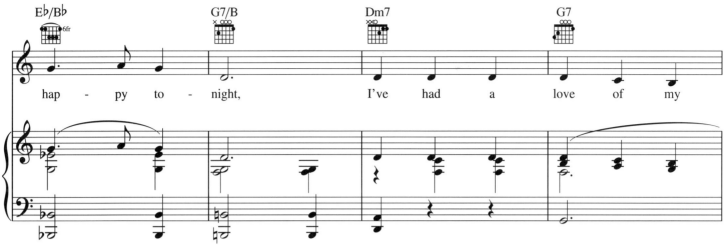

hap - py to - night, I've had a love of my

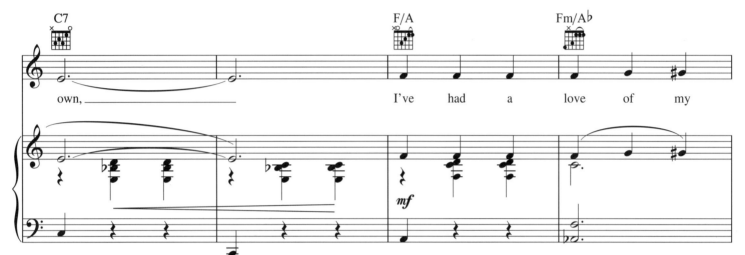

own, _____ I've had a love of my

own, like yours, I've had a love of my

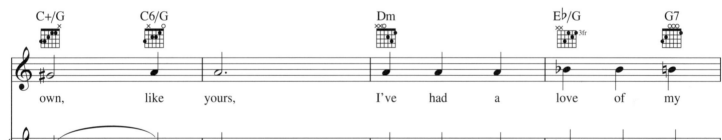

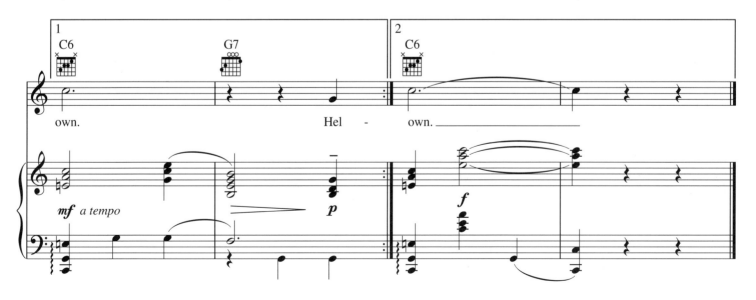

own. Hel - own. _____

I CAN'T HELP IT
(If I'm Still in Love with You)

Words and Music by
HANK WILLIAMS

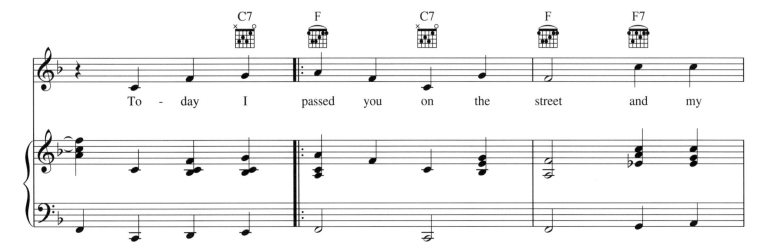

To-day I passed you on the street and my

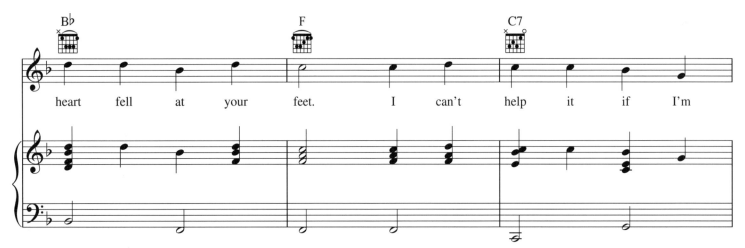

heart fell at your feet. I can't help it if I'm

still in love with you._____ Some-bod-y

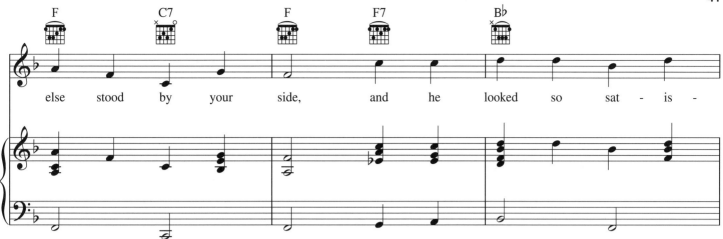

else stood by your side, and he looked so sat - is -

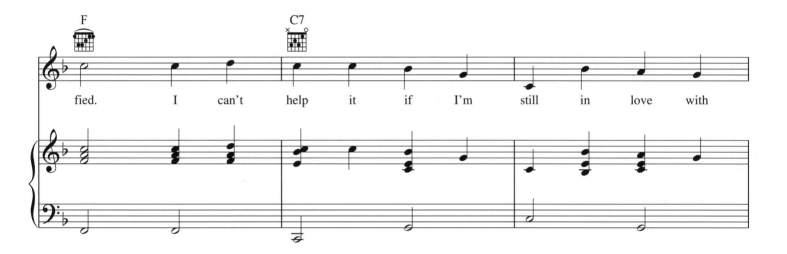

fied. I can't help it if I'm still in love with

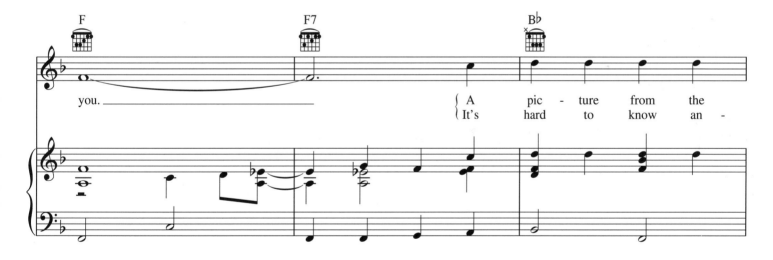

you. _____ { A pic - ture from the
{ It's hard to know an -

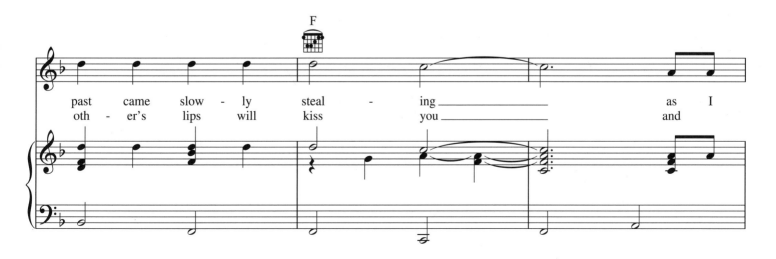

past came slow - ly steal - ing _____ as I
oth - er's lips will kiss you _____ and

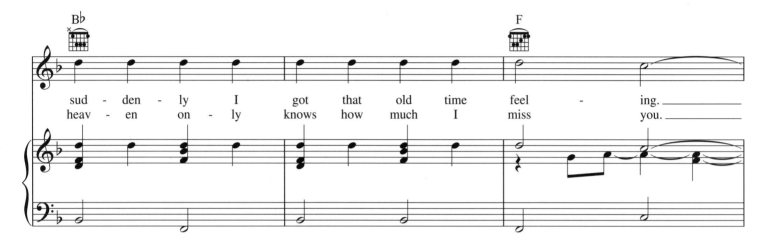

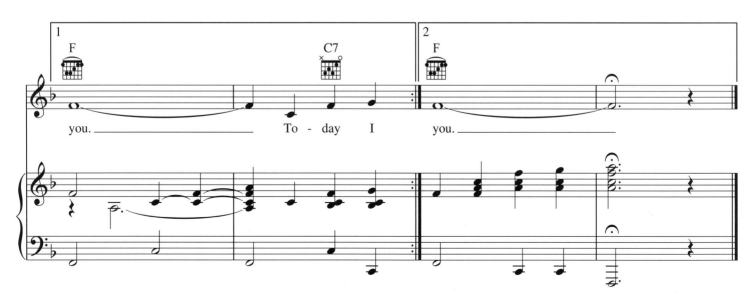

I LEFT MY HEART IN SAN FRANCISCO

Words by DOUGLASS CROSS
Music by GEORGE CORY

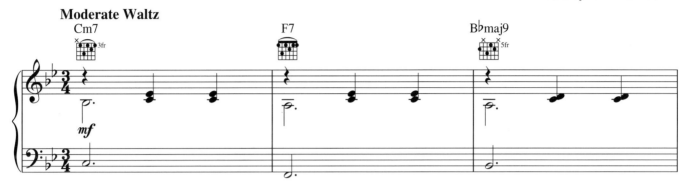

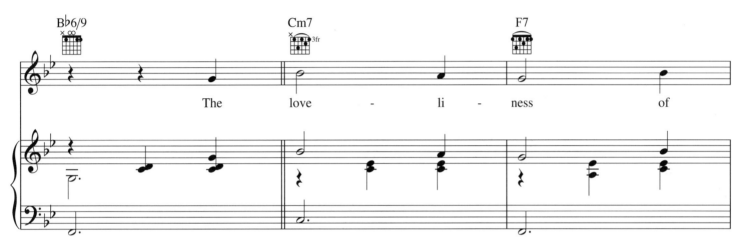

The love - li - ness of Par - is seems some - how

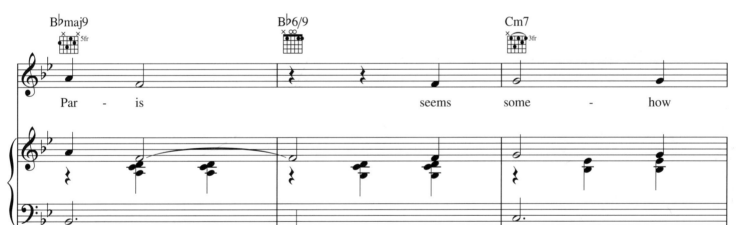

sad - ly gay. _____ The glo - ry

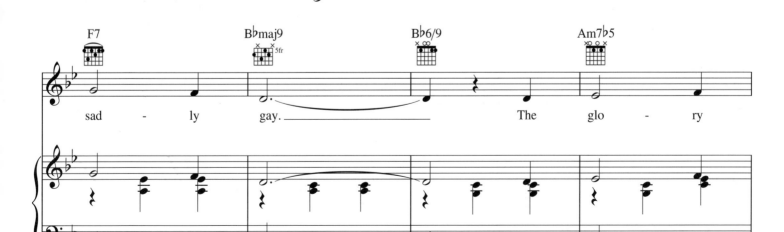

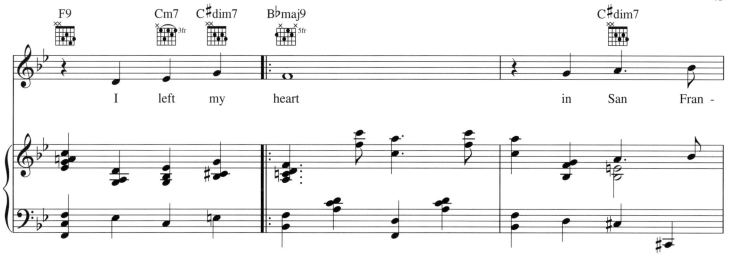

I left my heart in San Fran-

cis - co. _____ High on a hill,

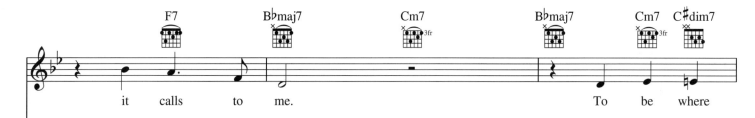

it calls to me. To be where

lit - tle ca - ble cars _____ climb half - way to the stars! _____

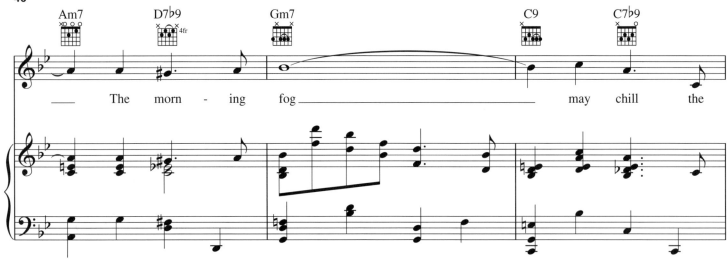

The morn - ing fog _____ may chill the

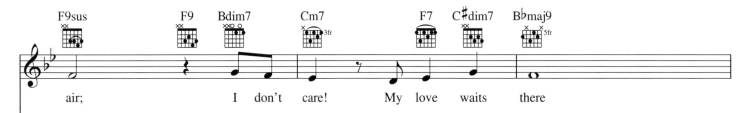

air; I don't care! My love waits there

in San Fran - cis - co, _____ a - bove the

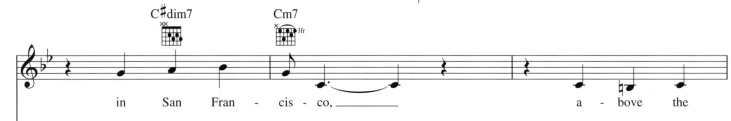

blue _____ and wind - y sea.

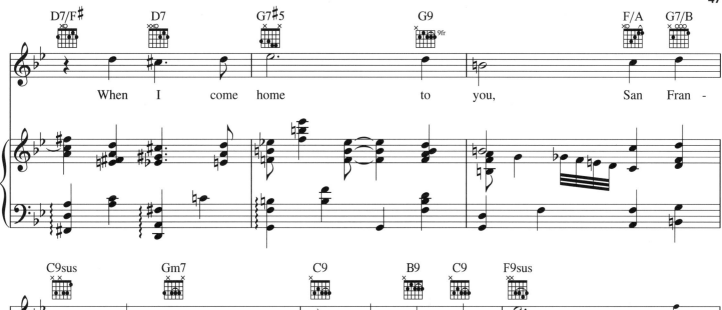

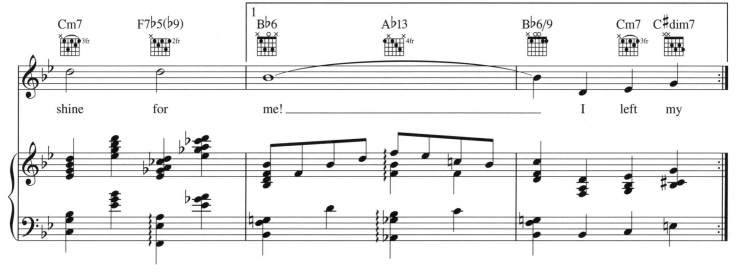

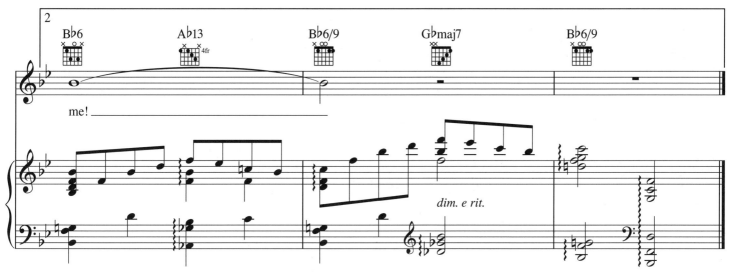

I HAVE DREAMED
from THE KING AND I

Lyrics by OSCAR HAMMERSTEIN II
Music by RICHARD RODGERS

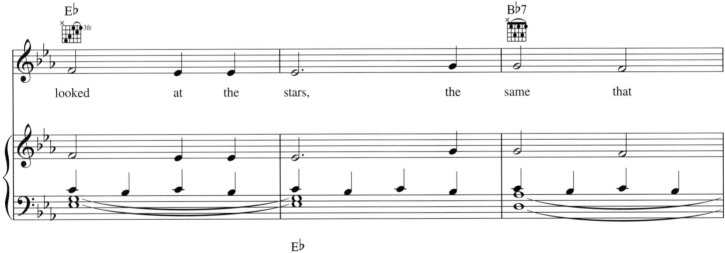

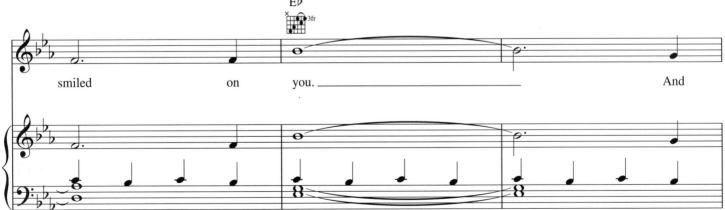

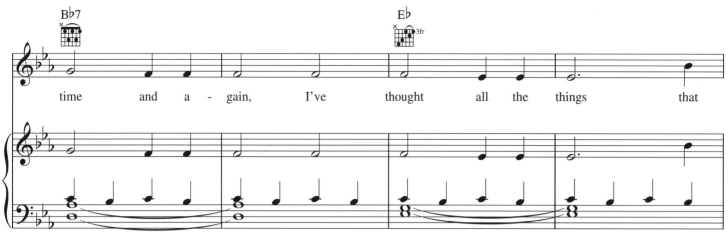

time and a - gain, I've thought all the things that

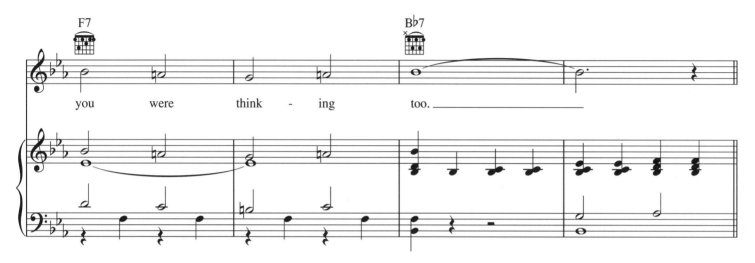

you were think - ing too.

I have dreamed that your arms are love - ly

I have dreamed what a joy you'll be.

view _____ In these dreams I've loved you so that by

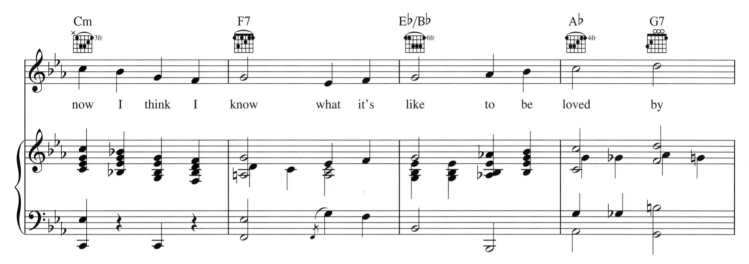

now I think I know what it's like to be loved by

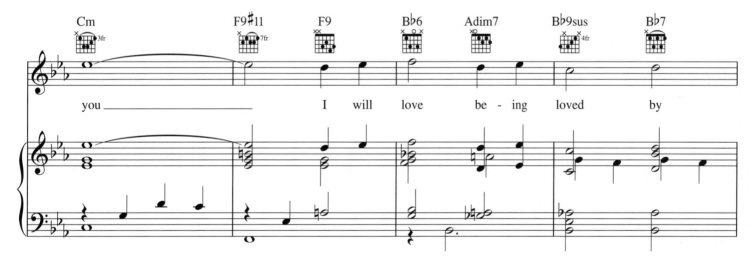

you _____ I will love be-ing loved by

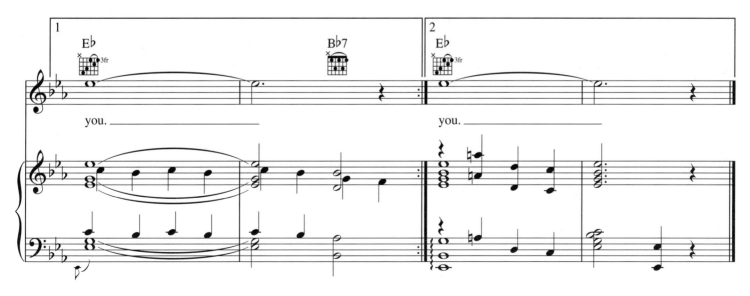

you. _____ you. _____

I WANT YOU, I NEED YOU, I LOVE YOU

Words by MAURICE MYSELS
Music by IRA KOSLOFF

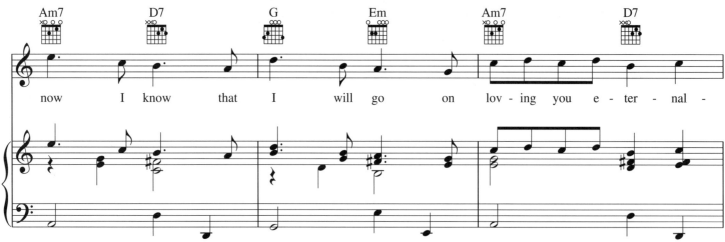

now I know that I will go on lov-ing you e-ter-nal -

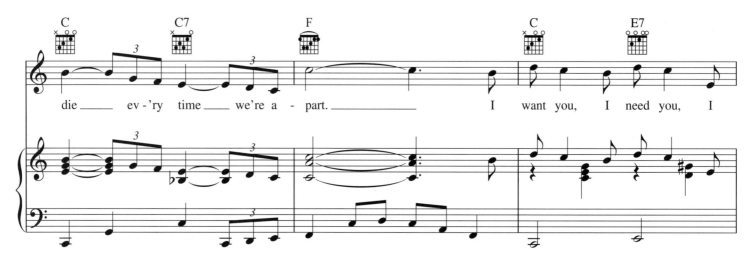

ly. Won't you please ___ be my own? ___ Nev-er leave ___ me a-lone, ___ 'cause I

die ___ ev-'ry time ___ we're a-part. _____ I want you, I need you, I

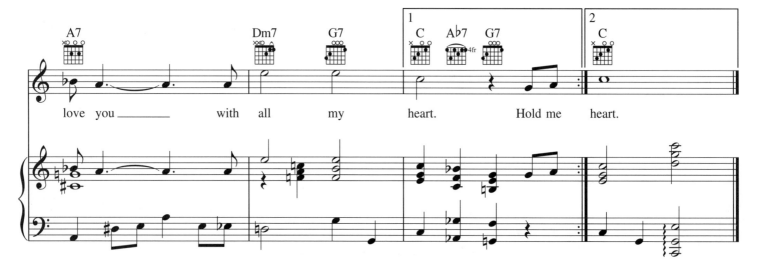

love you _____ with all my heart. Hold me heart.

IN THE WEE SMALL HOURS OF THE MORNING

Words by BOB HILLIARD
Music by DAVID MANN

Slowly, with restraint

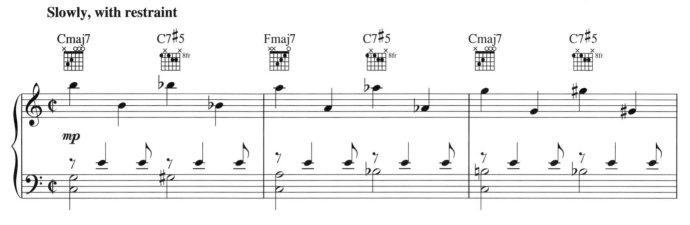

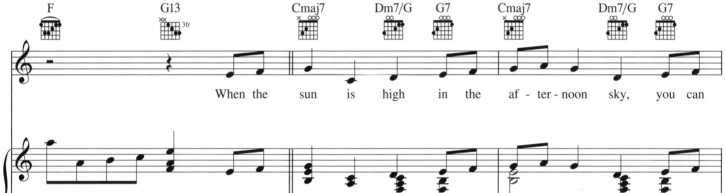

When the sun is high in the af-ter-noon sky, you can

al - ways find some-thing to do. But from dusk till dawn as the

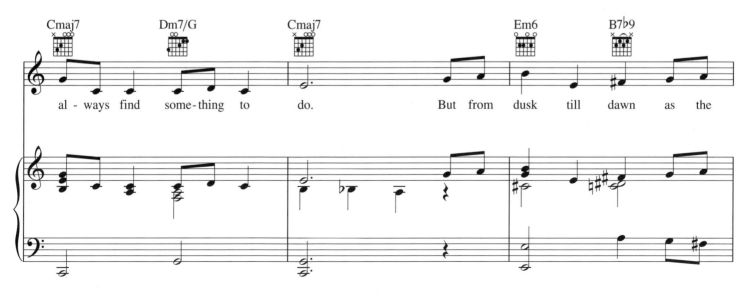

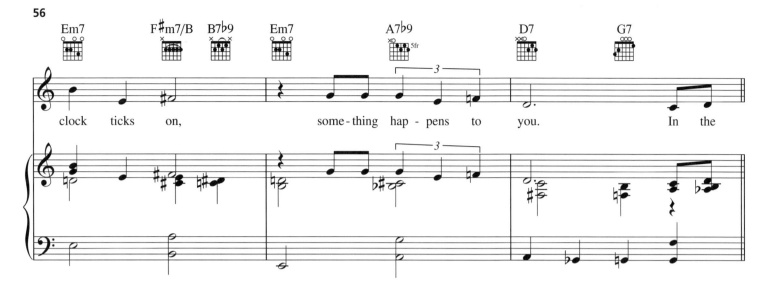

clock ticks on, some-thing hap-pens to you. In the

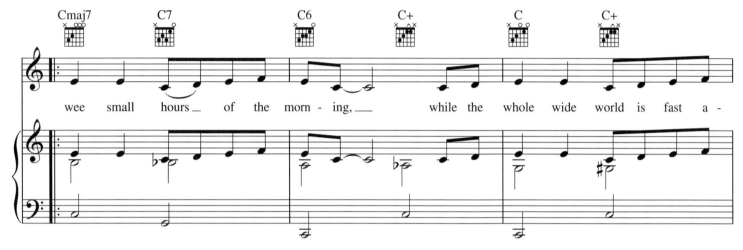

wee small hours __ of the morn-ing, ___ while the whole wide world is fast a-

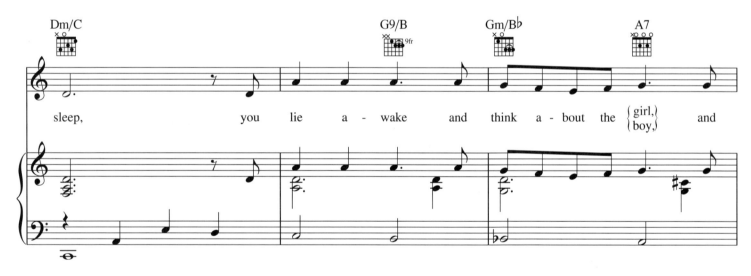

sleep, you lie a-wake and think a-bout the {girl,} {boy,} and

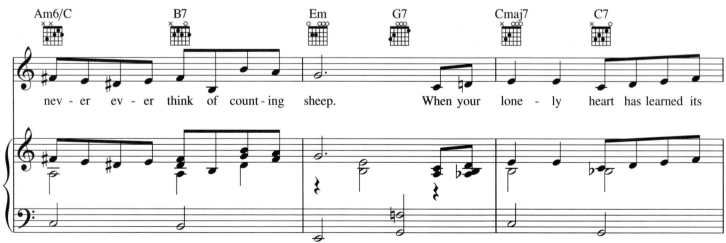

nev-er ev-er think of count-ing sheep. When your lone-ly heart has learned its

I'VE GROWN ACCUSTOMED TO HER FACE
from MY FAIR LADY

Words by ALAN JAY LERNER
Music by FREDERICK LOEWE

JUST IN TIME
from BELLS ARE RINGING

Words by BETTY COMDEN and ADOLPH GREEN
Music by JULE STYNE

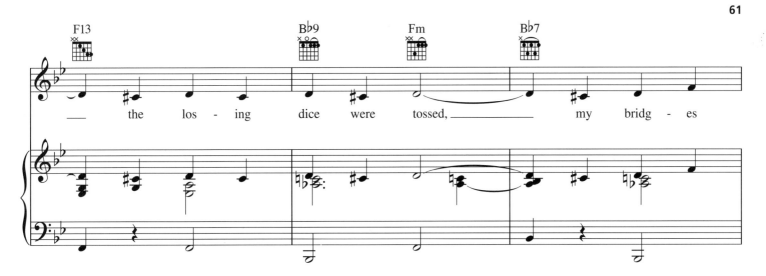

the los - ing dice were tossed, _____ my bridg - es

all were crossed, _____ no - where to go. _____

Now you're here, _____ and now I

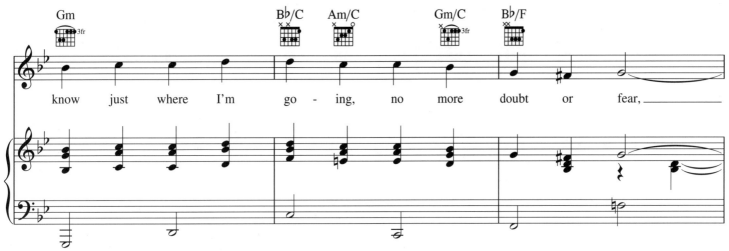

know just where I'm go - ing, no more doubt or fear, _____

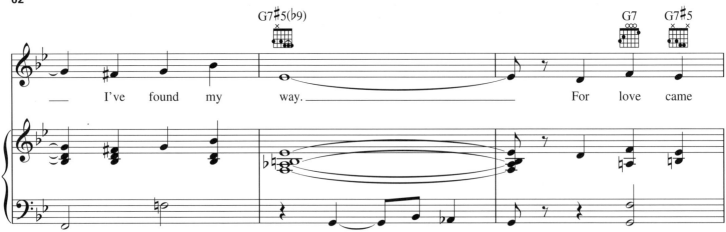

I've found my way. _____ For love came

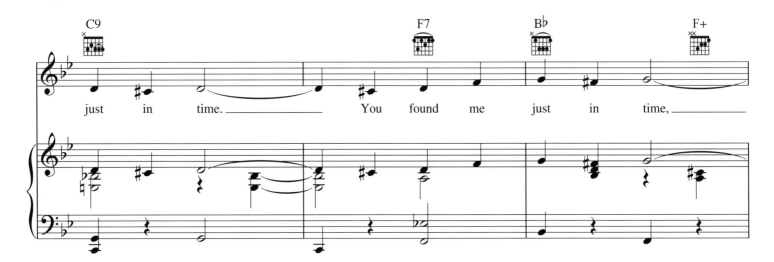

just in time. _____ You found me just in time, _____

____ and changed my lone - ly life, that love - ly

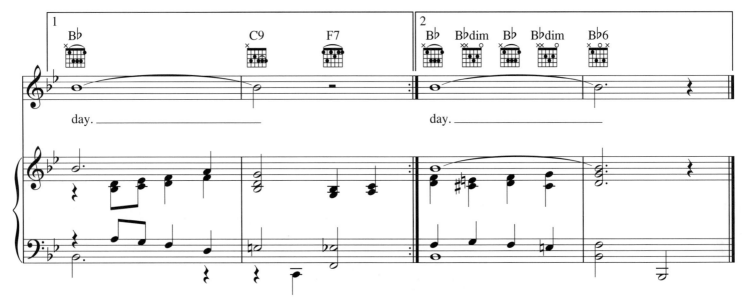

day. _____   day. _____

LOVE LETTERS IN THE SAND

Words by NICK KENNY and CHARLES KENNY
Music by J. FRED COOTS

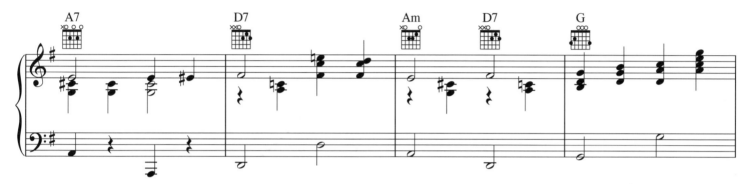

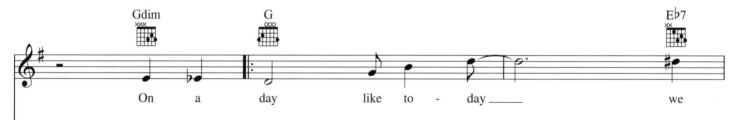

On a day like to-day ____ we

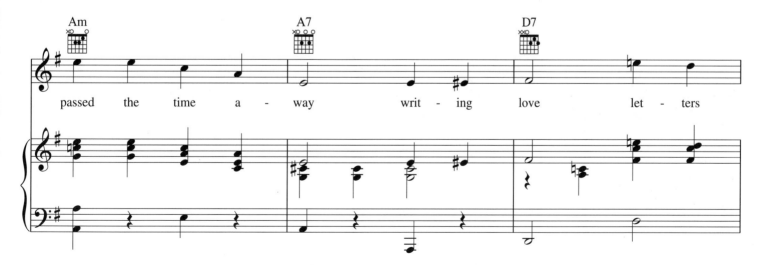

passed the time a - way writ-ing love let - ters

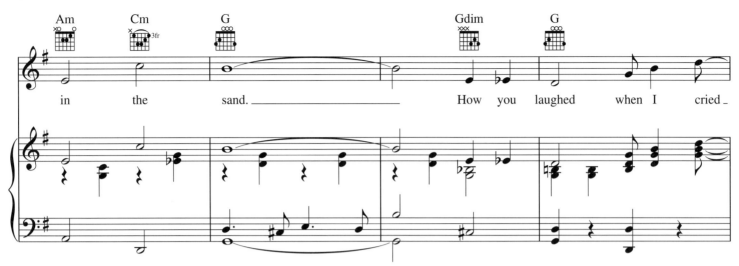

in the sand. _____ How you laughed when I cried _

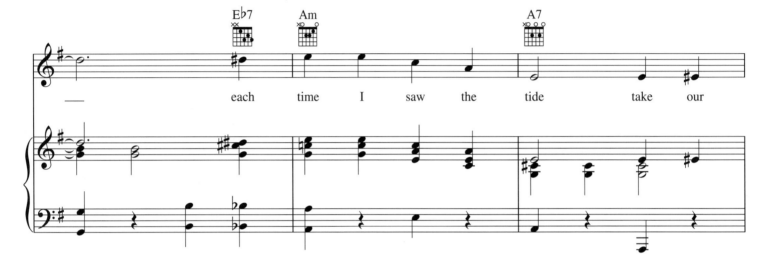

_ each time I saw the tide take our

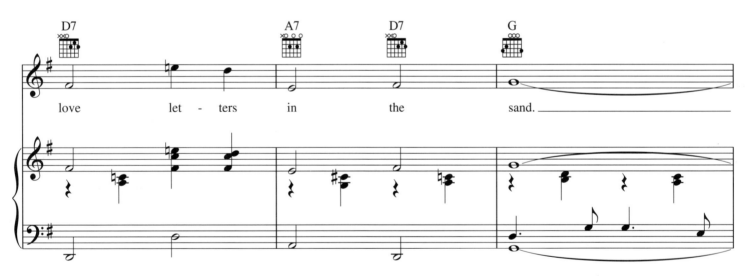

love let - ters in the sand. _____

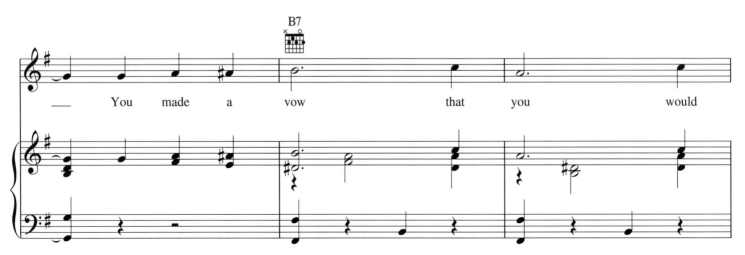

_ You made a vow that you would

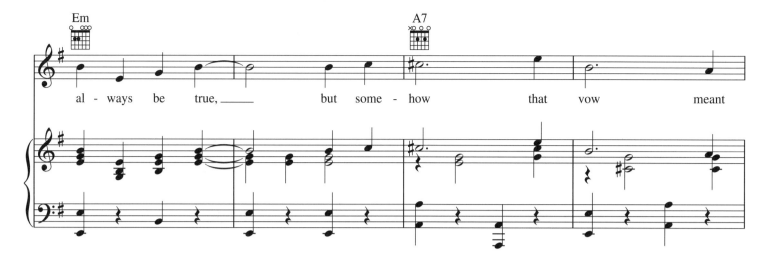

al - ways be true, _____ but some - how that vow meant

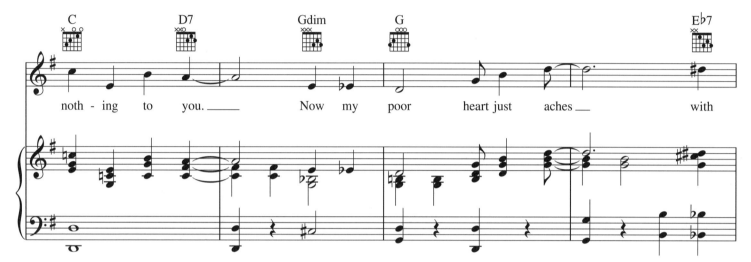

noth - ing to you. _____ Now my poor heart just aches _____ with

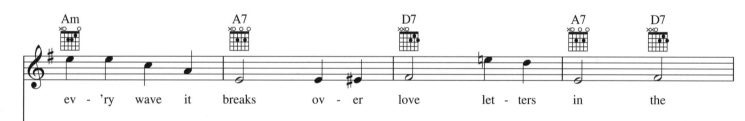

ev - 'ry wave it breaks ov - er love let - ters in the

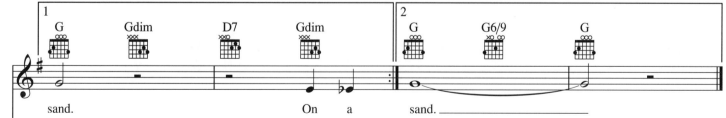

sand. On a sand. _____

LOVE ME TENDER

from LOVE ME TENDER

Words and Music by ELVIS PRESLEY
and VERA MATSON

Moderately slow

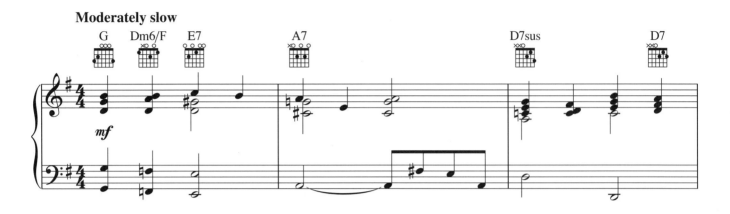

Love me ten - der, love me sweet,
Love me ten - der, love me long,
Love me ten - der, love me dear,
When at last my dreams come true,

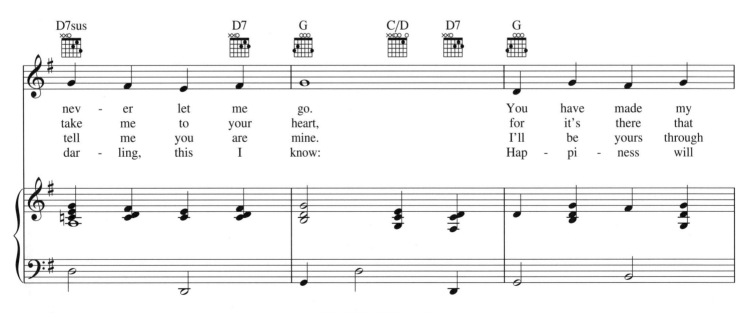

nev - er let me go.
take me to your heart,
tell me you are mine.
dar - ling, this I know:

You have made my
for it's made there that
I'll be yours through
Hap - pi - ness will

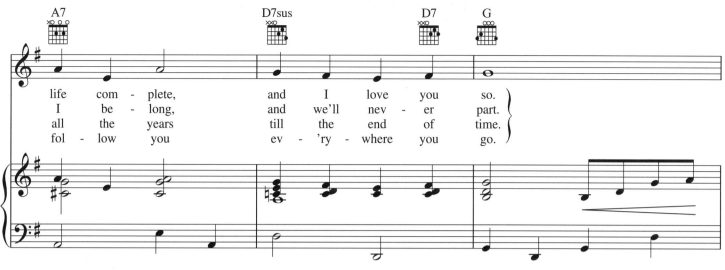

life com - plete, and I love you so.
I be - long, and we'll nev - er so part.
all the years till the end of time.
fol - low you ev - 'ry - where you go.

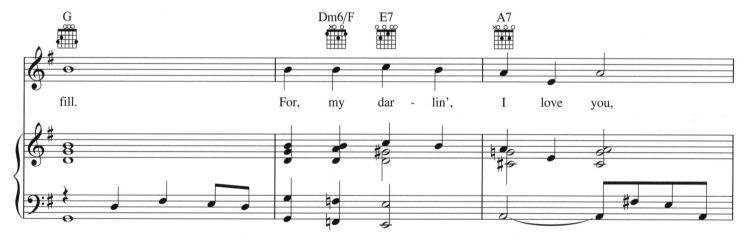

Love me ten - der, love me true, all my dreams ful -

fill. For, my dar - lin', I love you,

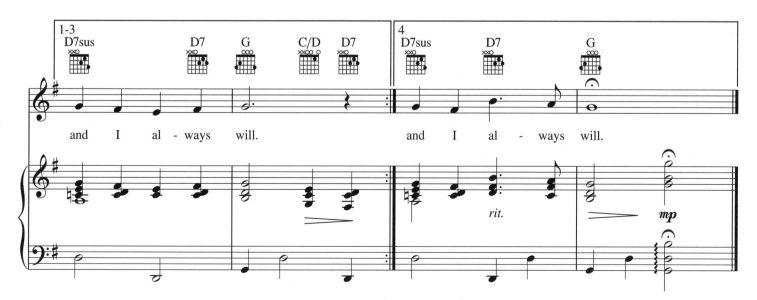

and I al - ways will. and I al - ways will.

LOVING YOU

Words and Music by JERRY LEIBER
and MIKE STOLLER

* Even eighth notes

MAGIC MOMENTS

Lyric by HAL DAVID
Music by BURT BACHARACH

Mag - ic mo - ments, mem - 'ries we've been

shar - ing. Mag - ic mo - ments,

when two hearts are car - ing. Time can't e -

rase the mem - 'ry of these mag - ic

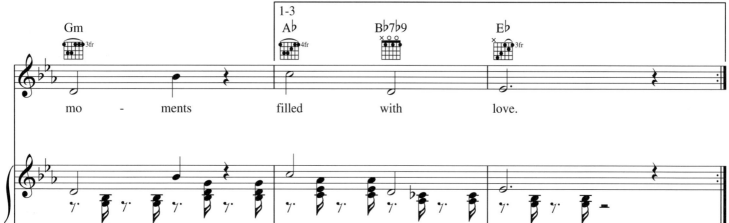

mo - ments filled with love.

filled with love. _____

(You've Got)
THE MAGIC TOUCH

Words and Music by
BUCK RAM

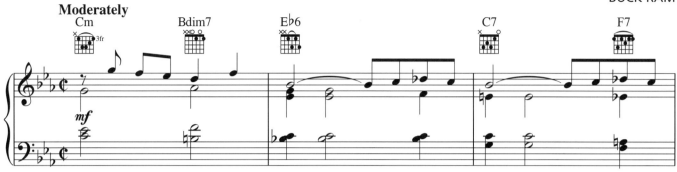

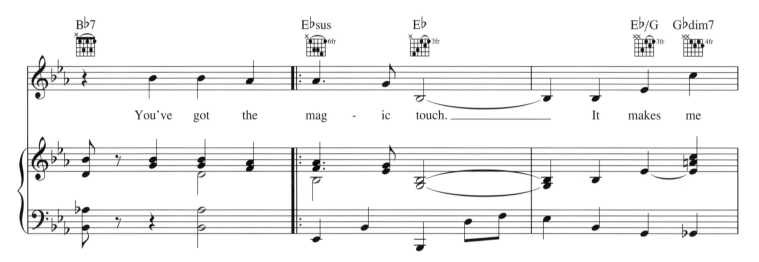

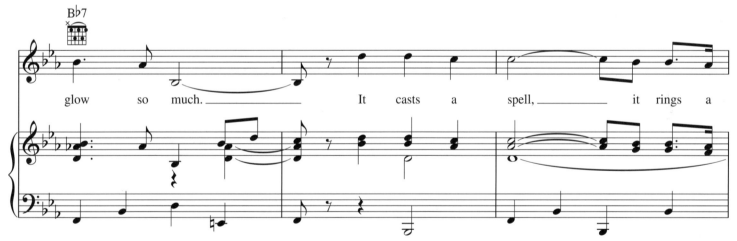

You've got the mag-ic touch._____ It makes me

glow so much._____ It casts a spell,_____ it rings a

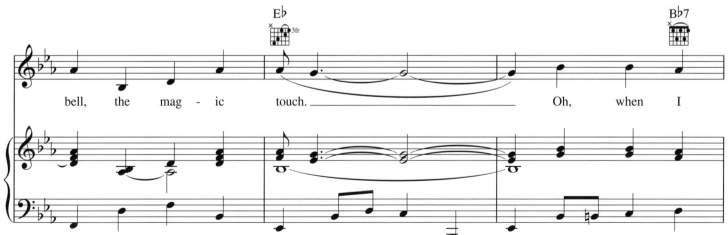

bell, the mag-ic touch._____ Oh, when I

feel your charm, _____ it's like a four - a - larm. _____

_____ You make me thrill so much, you've got the mag - ic

touch. _____ Here I go reel - ing, ____ oh,

oh. I'm feel - ing ____ the glow, but where can I

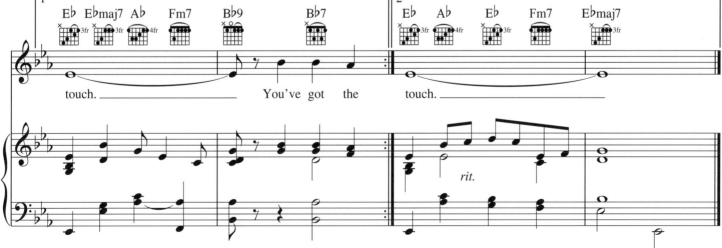

MEMORIES ARE MADE OF THIS

Words and Music by RICHARD DEHR,
FRANK MILLER and TERRY GILKYSON

One girl, one boy;

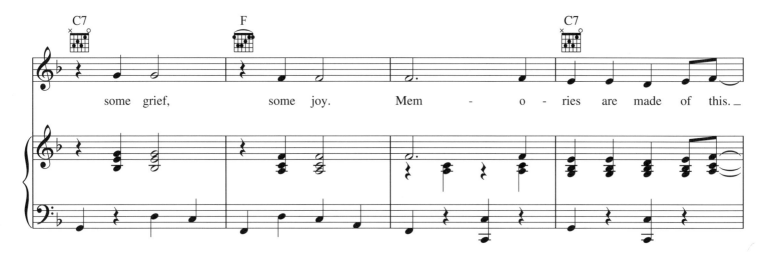

some grief, some joy. Mem - o - ries are made of this. _

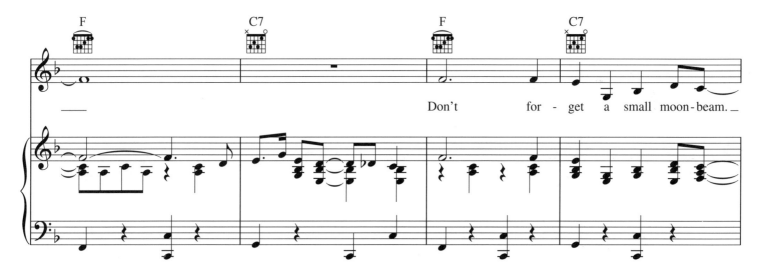

Don't for - get a small moon - beam. _

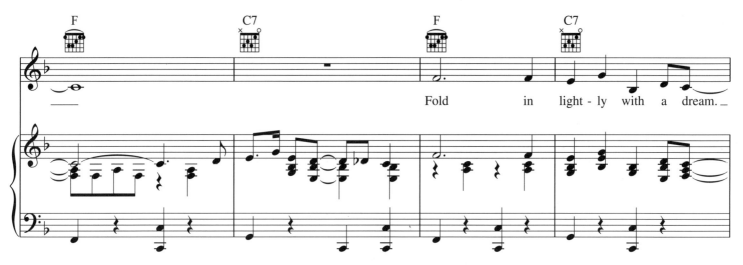

Fold in light - ly with a dream. _

Your lips and mine;

two sips of wine. Mem - o - ries are made of this. __

Then add the wed - ding bells, __

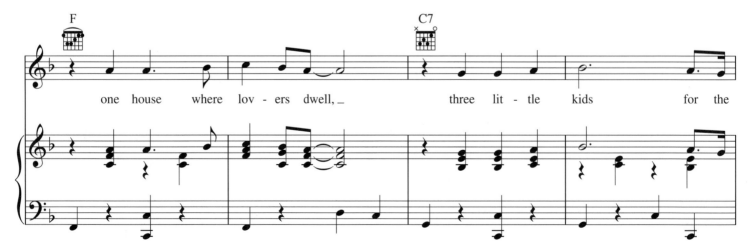

one house where lov - ers dwell, __ three lit - tle kids for the

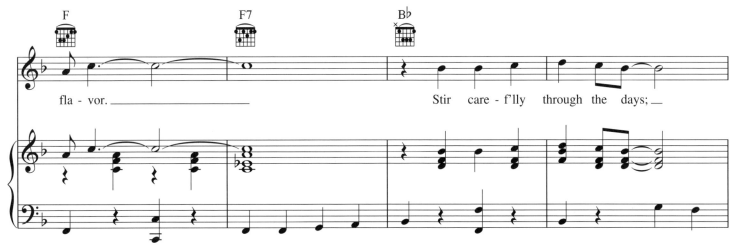

fla - vor. _____ Stir care - f'lly through the days; __

see how the fla - vor stays. These are the dreams you will

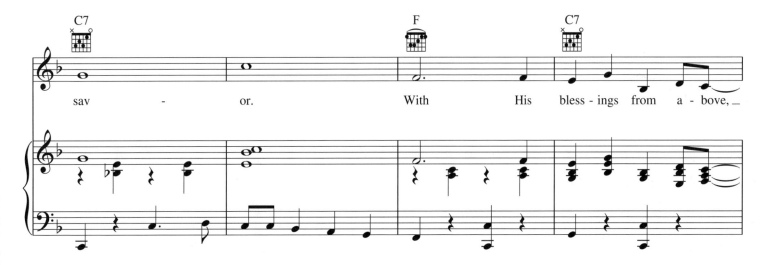

sav - or. With His bless - ings from a - bove, __

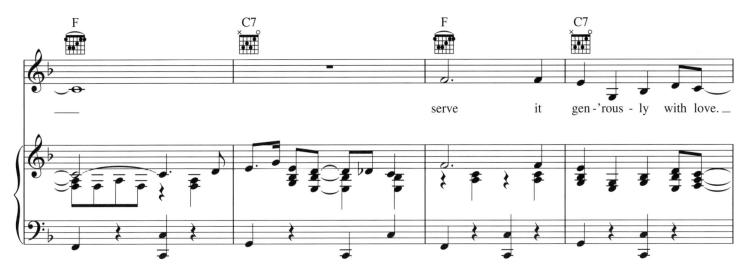

serve it gen -'rous - ly with love. __

One man, one wife;

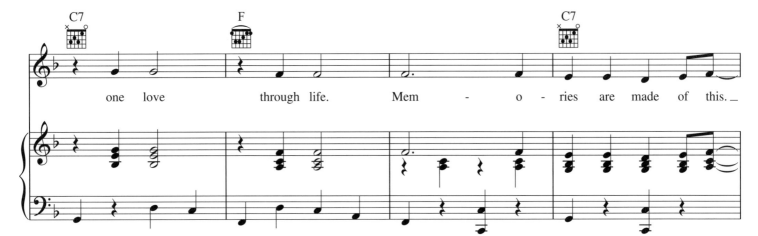

one love through life. Mem - o - ries are made of this.

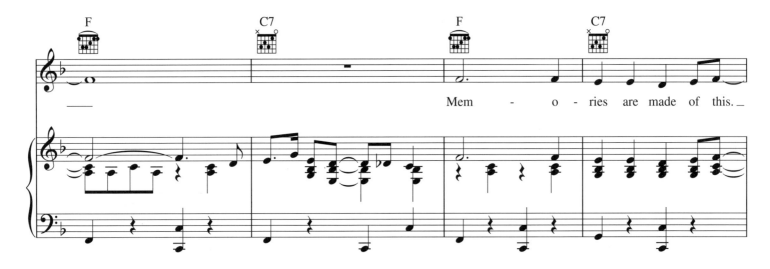

Mem - o - ries are made of this.

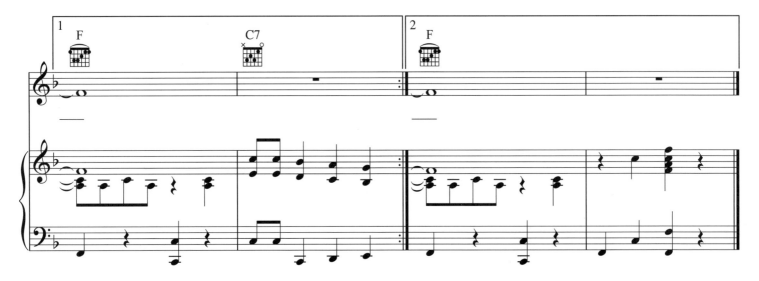

MISTY

Words by JOHNNY BURKE
Music by ERROLL GARNER

thou-sand vi - o - lins be - gin to play, Or it might be the sound of your hel - lo, That

mu - sic I hear, ___ I get mist - y, the mo - ment you're near.

You can say that you're lead - ing me on, ___ But it's just what I

want you to do, ___ Don't you no - tice how hope - less - ly I'm lost, ___

MOMENTS TO REMEMBER

Words by AL STILLMAN
Music by ROBERT ALLEN

Moderately slow

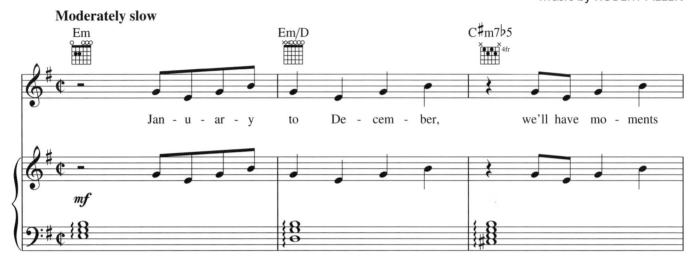

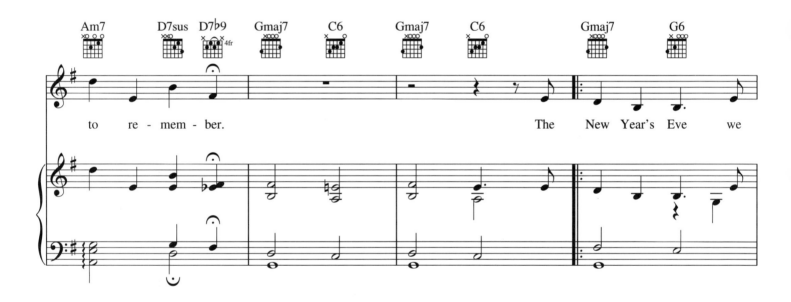

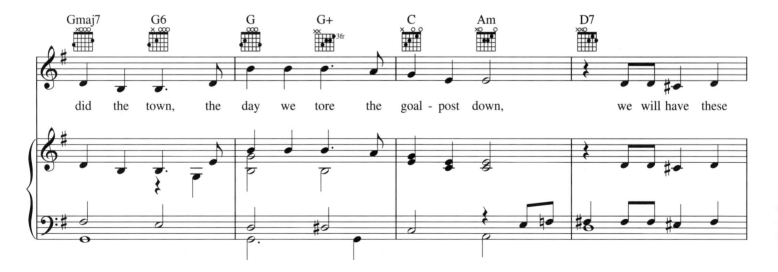

moments to re-mem-ber. The qui-et walks, the

nois-y fun, the ball-room prize we al-most won, we will have these

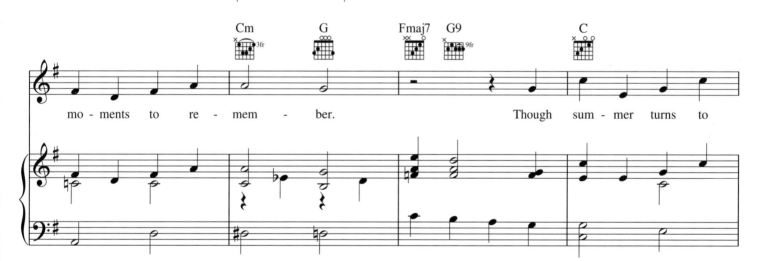

mo-ments to re-mem-ber. Though sum-mer turns to

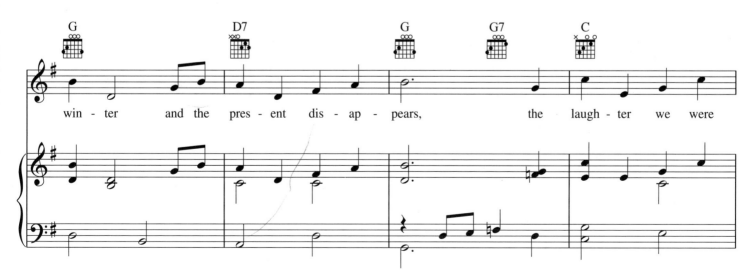

win-ter and the pres-ent dis-ap-pears, the laugh-ter we were

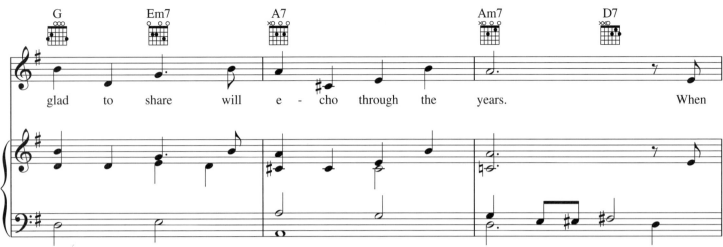

glad to share will e - cho through the years. When

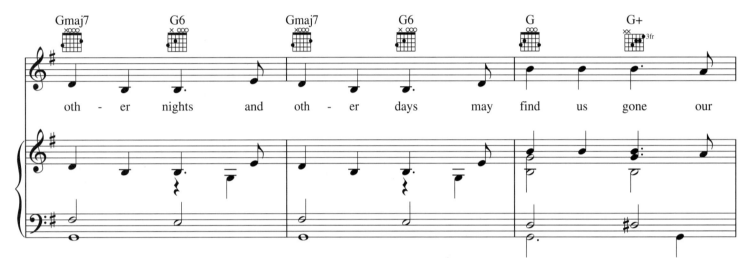

oth - er nights and oth - er days may find us gone our

sep - 'rate ways, we will have these mo - ments to re -

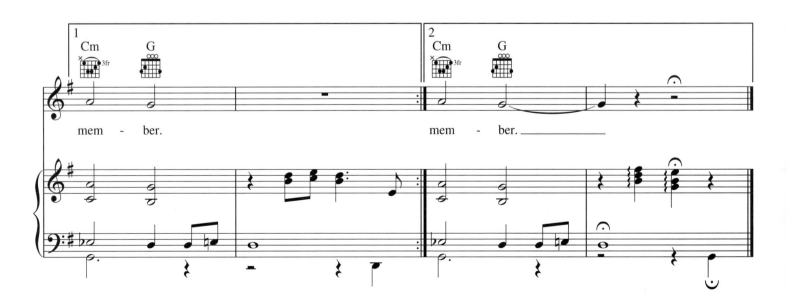

mem - ber. mem - ber.

MY ONE AND ONLY LOVE

Words by ROBERT MELLIN
Music by GUY WOOD

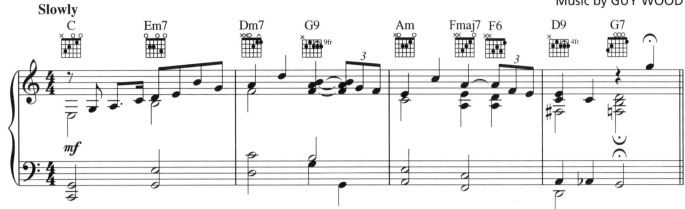

The ver - y thought of you makes my heart sing ___ like an A - pril breeze ___ on the

wings of spring, and you ap - pear in all your splen - dor, ___

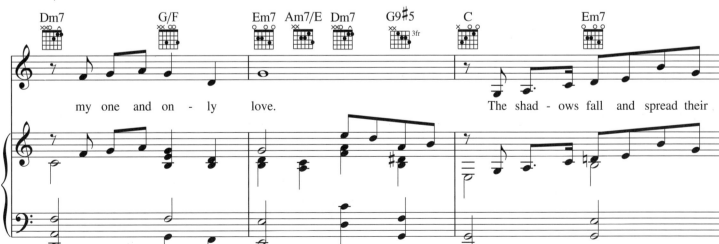

my one and on - ly love. The shad - ows fall and spread their

mys - tic charms ___ in the hush of night ___ while you're in my arms.

I feel your lips so warm and ten - der, ___ my one and on - ly

love. The touch ___ of your hand ___ is like heav - en, ___ a

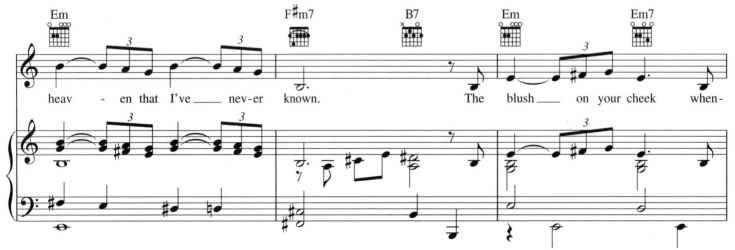

heav - en that I've ___ nev-er known. The blush ___ on your cheek when-

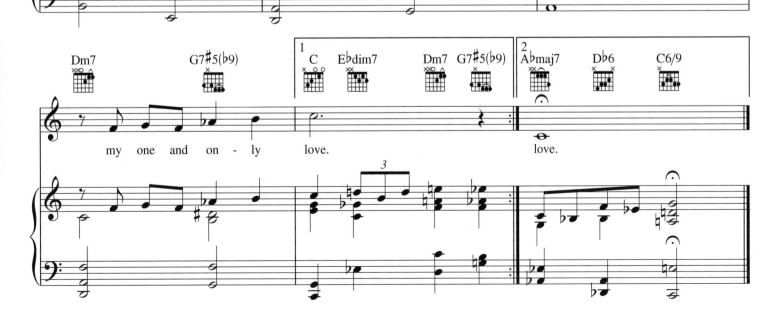

NEVER LET ME GO

from the Paramount Picture THE SCARLET HOUR

Words and Music by JAY LIVINGSTON
and RAY EVANS

out you! ____ Nev - er let me go! I'd be so lost if

you __ went a - way. ____ There'd be a thou-sand hours _ in the day ____

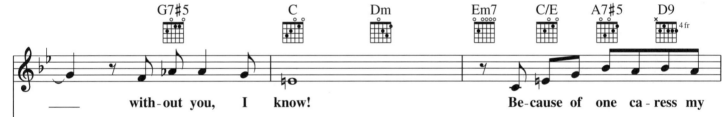

___ with-out you, I know! Be-cause of one ca-ress my

world was o - ver-turned at the ver - y start; All my bridg-es burned

NEVERTHELESS
(I'm in Love with You)

Words and Music by BERT KALMAR
and HARRY RUBY

Maybe I'll win __ and may-be I'll lose, __ and may-be I'm in __ for

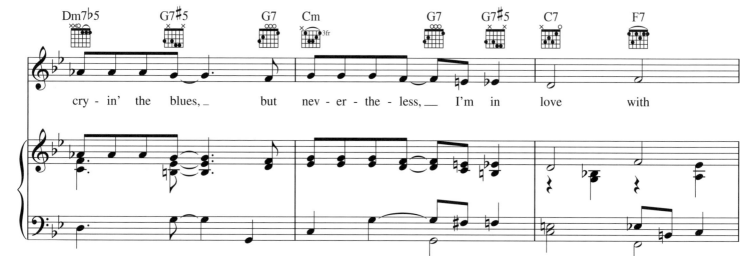

cry-in' the blues, __ but nev-er-the-less, __ I'm in love with

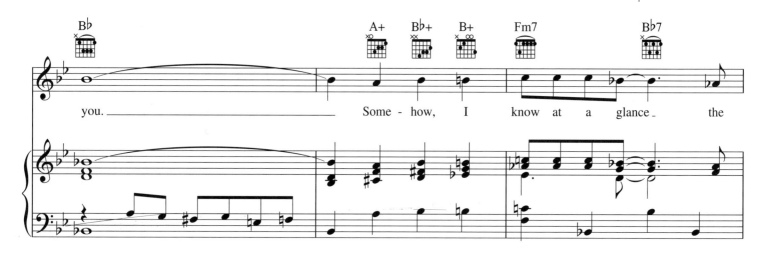

you. _____ Some-how, I know at a glance __ the

ter-ri-ble chanc-es I'm tak - ing:

fine at the start, __ then left with a heart __ that is break -

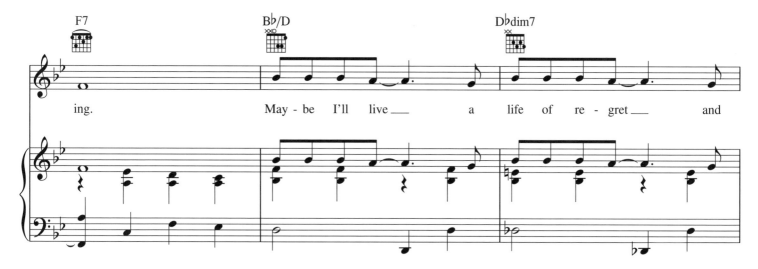

ing. May - be I'll live __ a life of re - gret __ and

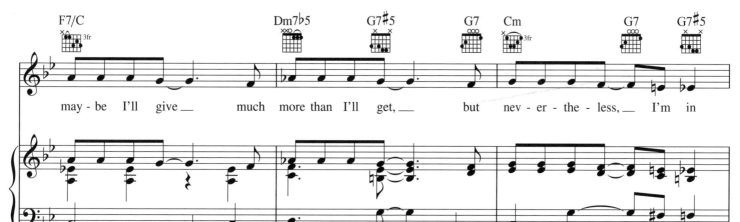

may - be I'll give __ much more than I'll get, __ but nev - er - the - less, __ I'm in

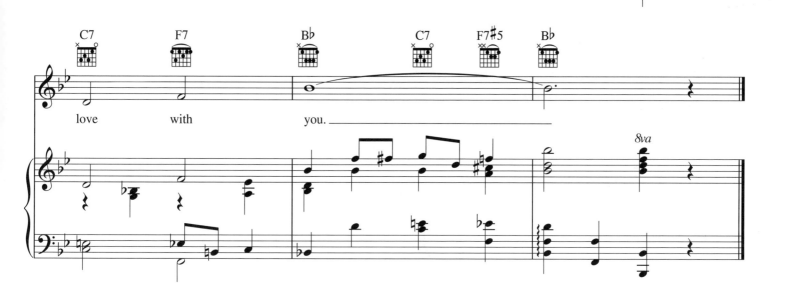

love with you. _____

ON THE STREET WHERE YOU LIVE

from MY FAIR LADY

Words by ALAN JAY LERNER
Music by FREDERICK LOEWE

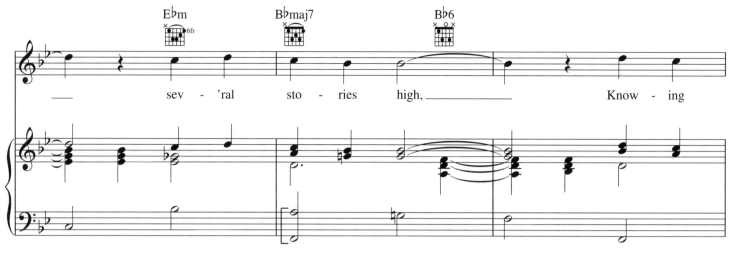

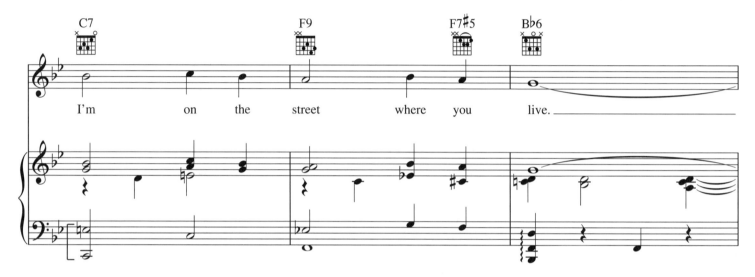

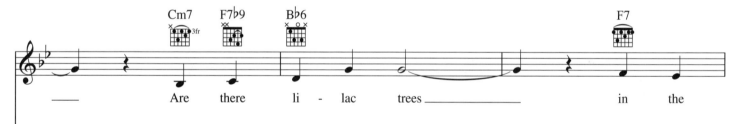

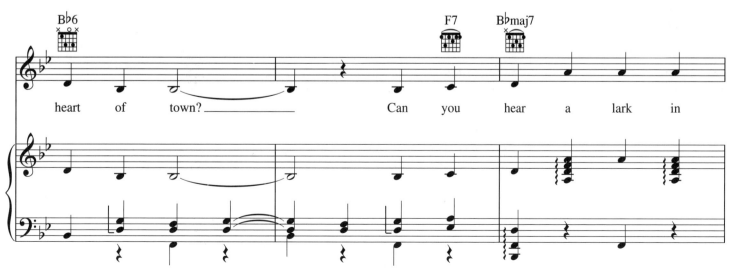

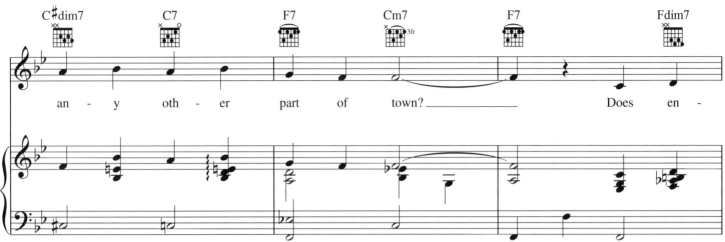

an - y oth - er part of town? _____ Does en -

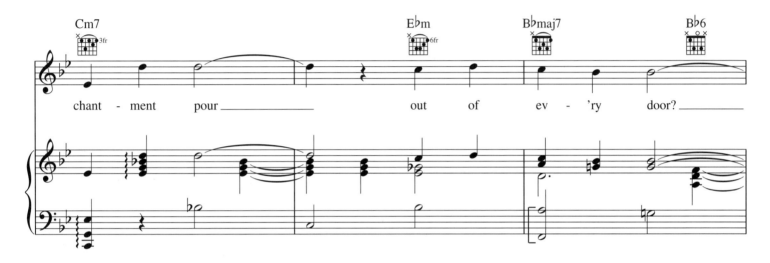

chant - ment pour _____ out of ev - 'ry door? _____

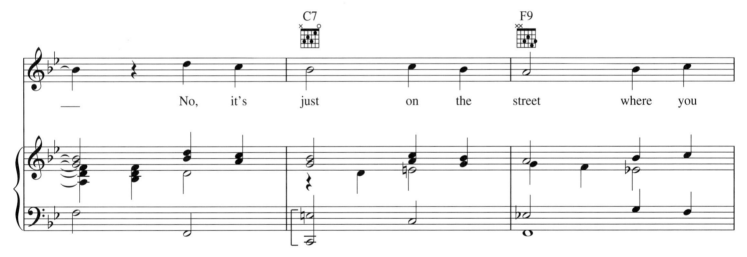

___ No, it's just on the street where you

live. _____ And oh, _____ the tow - er - ing

feel - ing, _____ Just to know _____

___ some - how you are near! _____ The o -

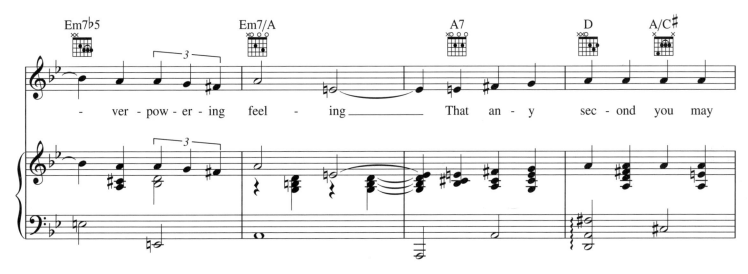

- ver - pow - er - ing feel - ing _____ That an - y sec - ond you may

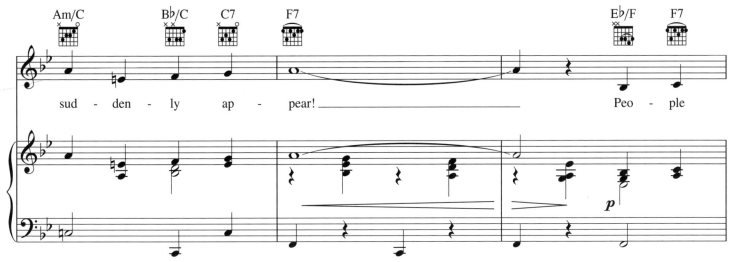

sud - den - ly ap - pear! _____ Peo - ple

STRANGER IN PARADISE

from KISMET

Words and Music by ROBERT WRIGHT
and GEORGE FORREST
(Music Based on Themes of A. Borodin)

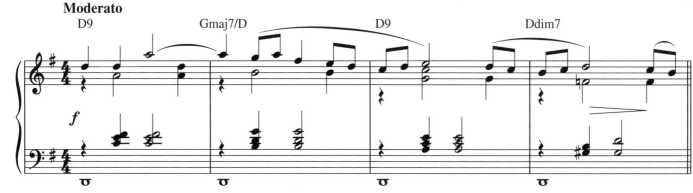

Take my hand, _____ I'm a stran-ger in par-a-dise, All lost in a

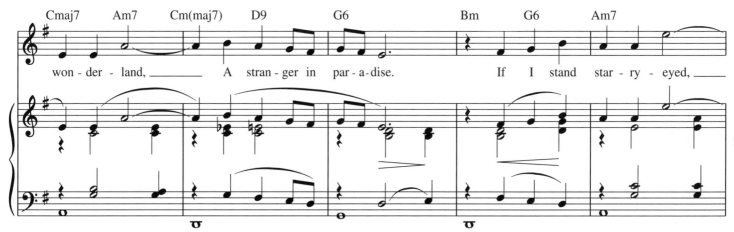

won-der-land, _____ A stran-ger in par-a-dise. If I stand star-ry-eyed, _____

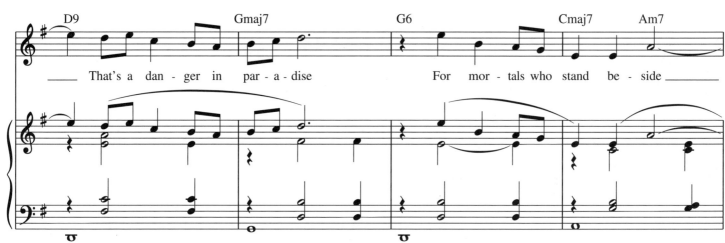

_____ That's a dan-ger in par-a-dise For mor-tals who stand be-side _____

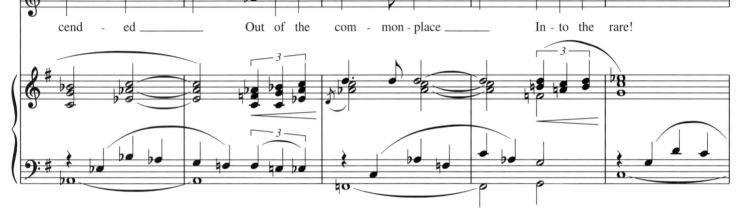

An an-gel like you. I saw your face _____ And I as-

cend - ed _____ Out of the com-mon-place _____ In-to the rare!

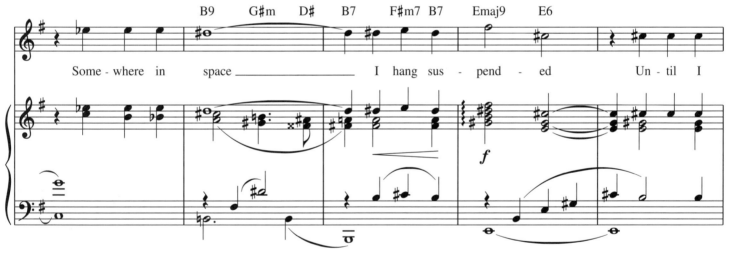

Some-where in space _____ I hang sus-pend - ed Un - til I

know _____ There's a chance that you care; Won't you an-swer the

ONLY YOU
(And You Alone)

Words and Music by BUCK RAM
and ANDE RAND

Slowly, with feeling

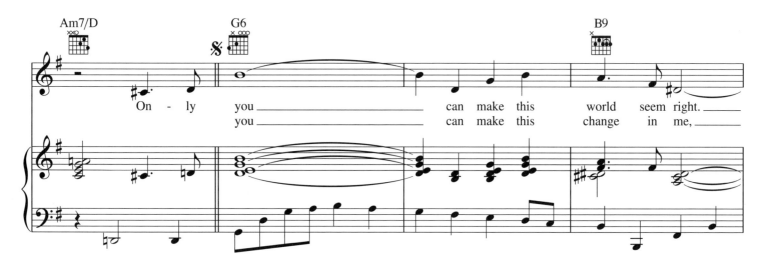

On-ly you _____ can make this world seem right. _____
you _____ can make this change in me, _____

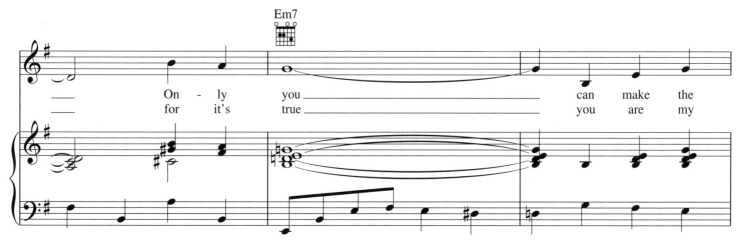

On-ly you _____ can make the
for it's true _____ you are my

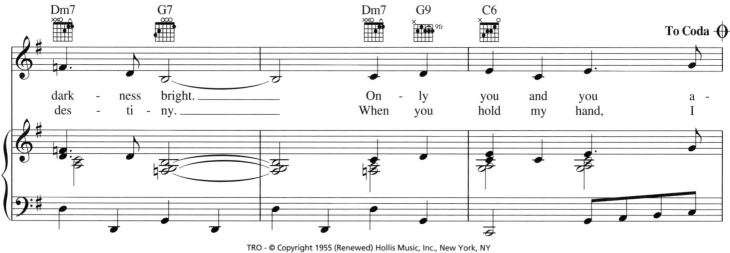

dark-ness bright. _____ On-ly you and you a-
des-ti-ny. _____ When you hold my hand, I

To Coda

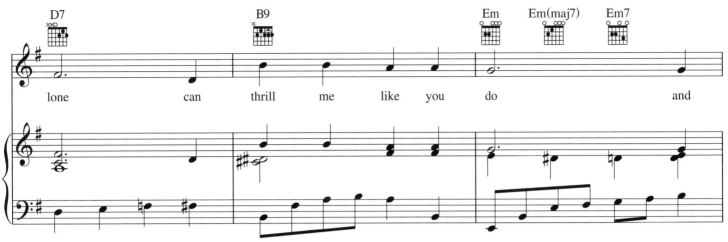

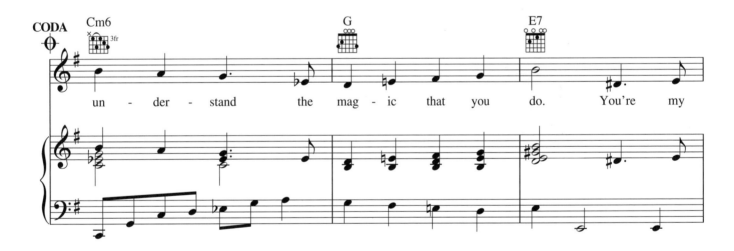

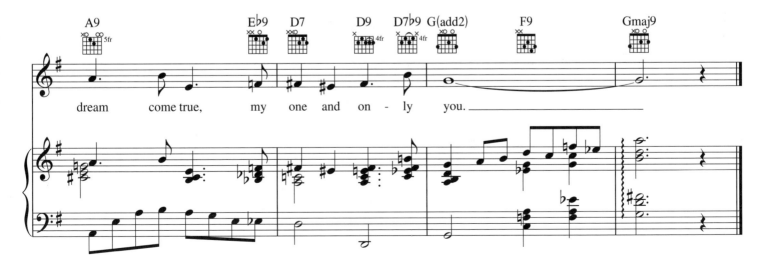

P.S. I LOVE YOU

Words by JOHNNY MERCER
Music by GORDON JENKINS

Gm7 **C7** **Fm7** **B♭7** **B♭m6/G** **C7**

rain, but all in all, I can't com - plain.

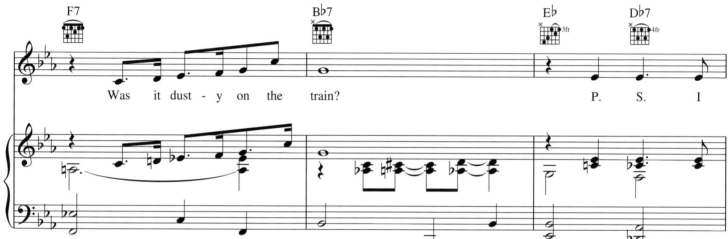

F7 **B♭7** **E♭** **D♭7**

Was it dust - y on the train? P. S. I

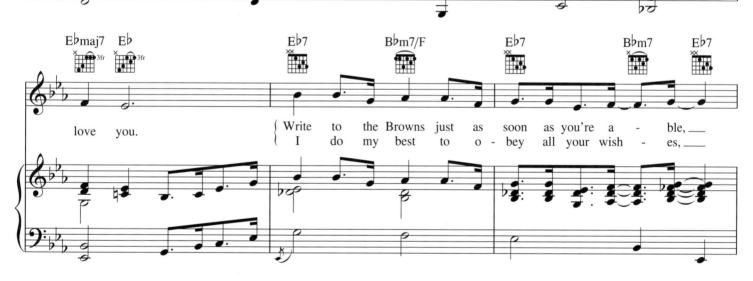

E♭maj7 **E♭** **E♭7** **B♭m7/F** **E♭7** **B♭m7** **E♭7**

love you.
{ Write to the Browns just as soon as you're a - ble, ___
{ I do my best to o - bey all your wish - es, ___

A♭ **F7/A** **Cm7/G**

They came a - round to call; ___ I burned a hole in the
I put a sign up THINK! _ But I got - ta buy us a

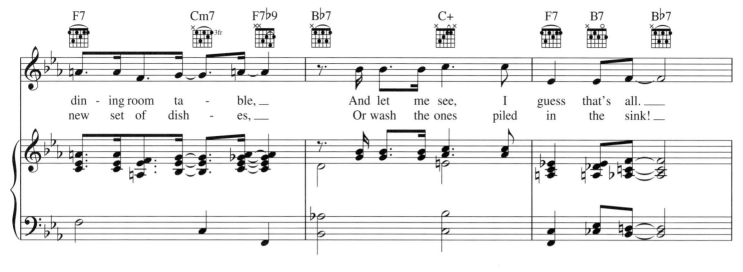

din - ing room ta - ble, __ And let me see, I guess that's all. __
new set of dish - es, __ Or wash the ones piled in the sink! __

Noth - ing else for me to say, And so I'll close, but, by the
Noth - ing else to tell you, dear, Ex - cept each day seems like a

way, Ev - 'ry - bod - y's think - ing of you. __
year, Ev - 'ry night I'm think - ing of you. __

P. S. I love you.
P. S. I love you.

PUT YOUR HEAD ON MY SHOULDER

Words and Music by
PAUL ANKA

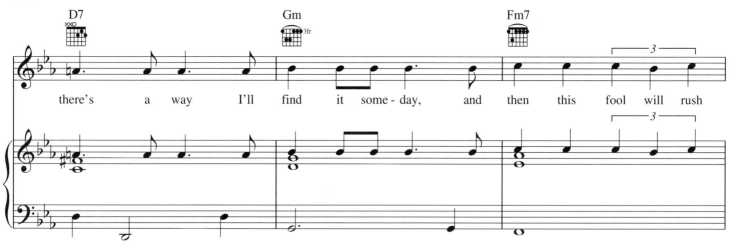

there's a way I'll find it some-day, and then this fool will rush

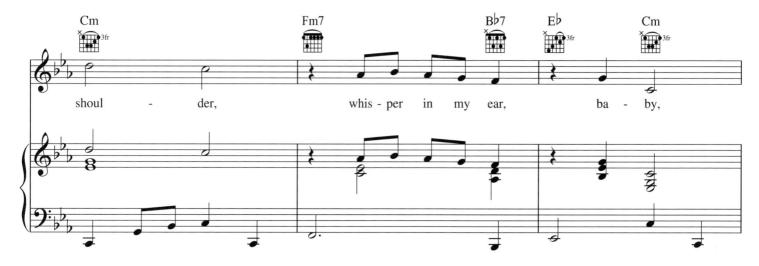

in. Put your head on my

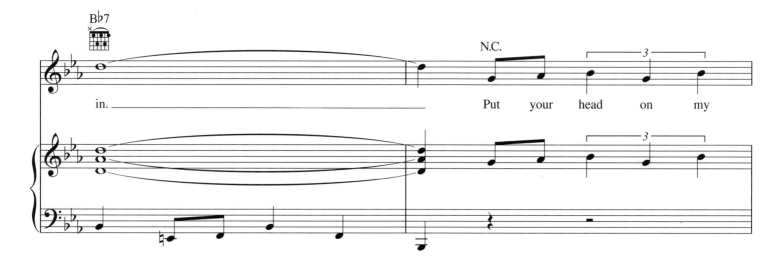

shoul - der, whis - per in my ear, ba - by,

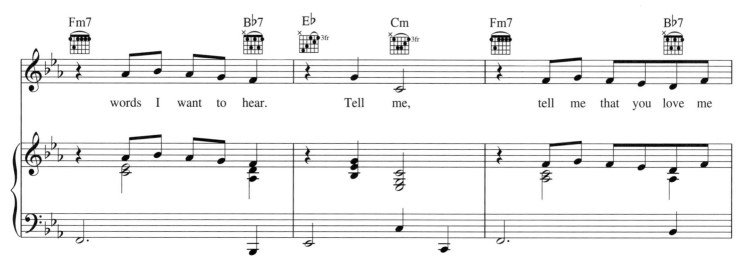

words I want to hear. Tell me, tell me that you love me

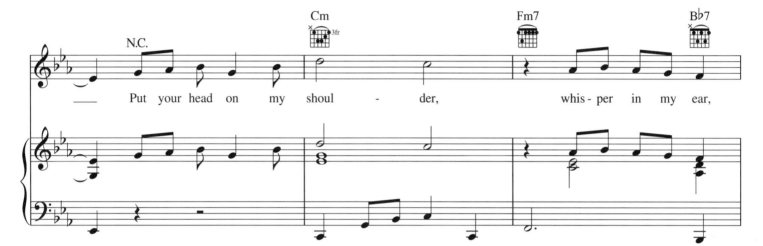

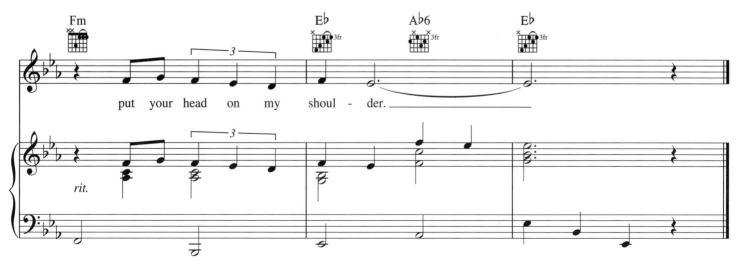

SEA OF LOVE

Words and Music by GEORGE KHOURY
and PHILIP BAPTISTE

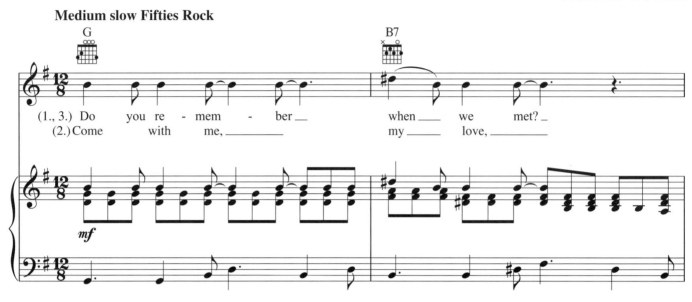

Medium slow Fifties Rock

(1., 3.) Do you re-mem-ber ___ when ___ we met? ___
(2.) Come with me, ___ my ___ love, ___

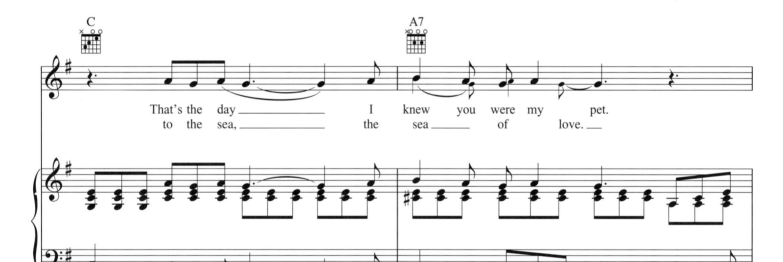

That's the day ___ I knew you were my pet.
to the sea, ___ the sea ___ of love. ___

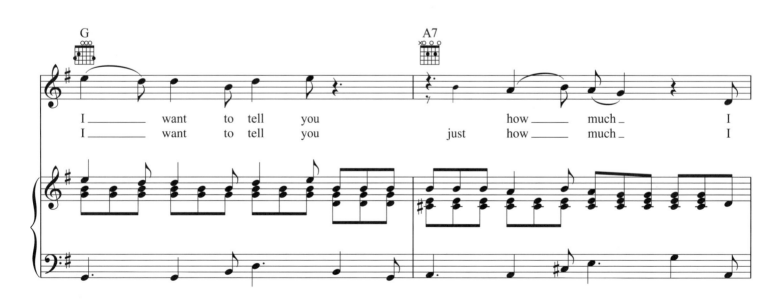

I ___ want to tell you ___ how ___ much ___ I
I ___ want to tell you just how ___ much ___ I

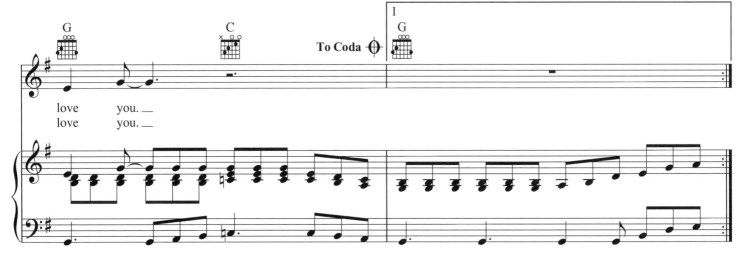

love you. —
love you. —

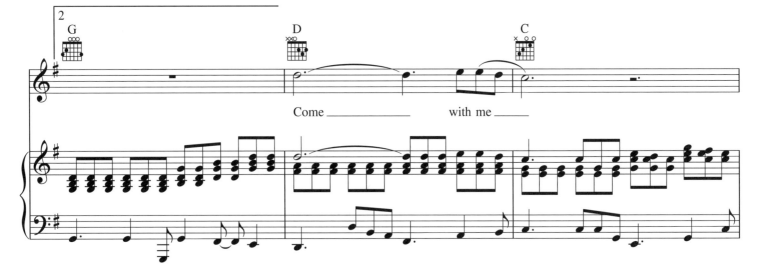

Come ———— with me ————

to ———— the sea ———— of

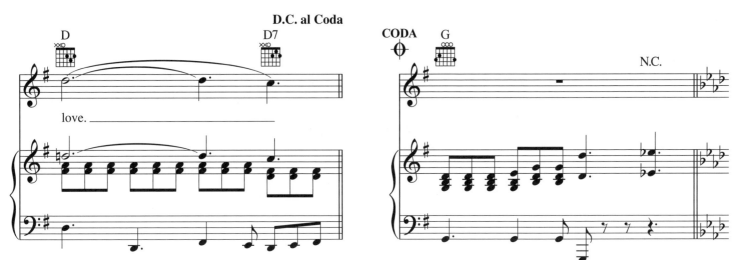

love. ————

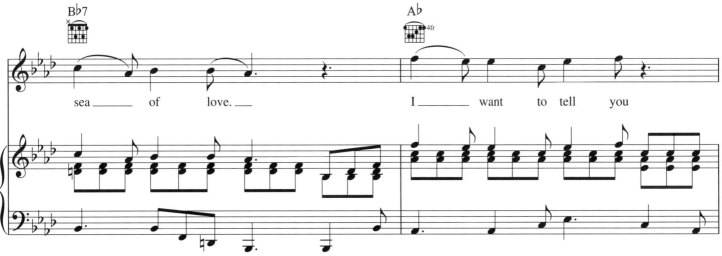

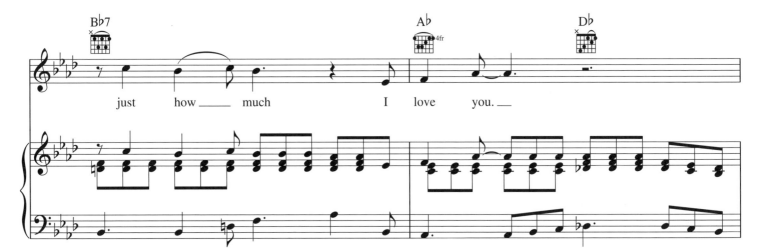

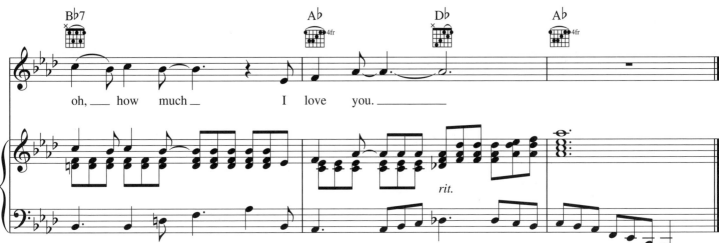

TEACH ME TONIGHT

Music by GENE DePAUL
Words by SAMMY CAHN

Did you say, "I've got a lot to learn?" _____ Well, don't think I'm try-ing

not to learn. Since this is the per-fect spot to learn,

teach me to-night. Start-ing with the "A, B,

love you" a thou-sand times a-cross the sky. One thing is-n't ver-y

clear, my love. _____ Should the teach-er stand so near, my love? _____

___ Grad-u-a-tion's al-most here, my love. Teach me to-night.

Did you say, "I've got a night. _____

THAT'S AMORÉ
(That's Love)
from the Paramount Picture THE CADDY

Words by JACK BROOKS
Music by HARRY WARREN

Moderately

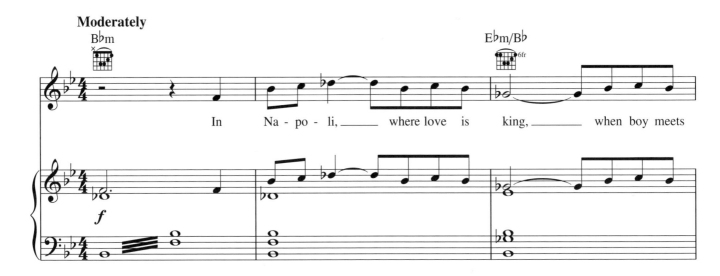

In Na- po- li, _____ where love is king, _____ when boy meets

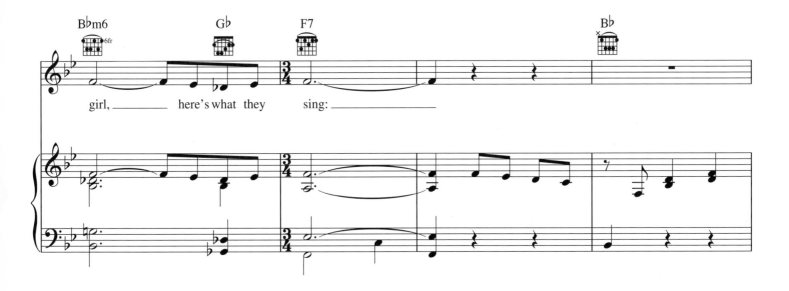

girl, _____ here's what they sing: _____

When the moon hits your eye like a

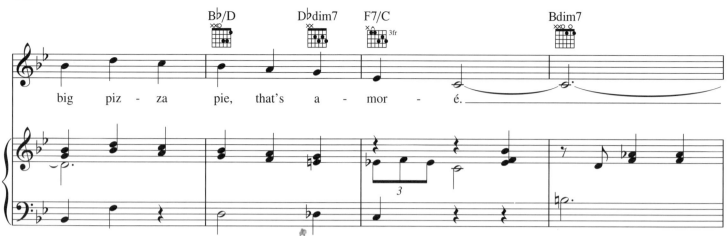

big piz - za pie, that's a - mor - é. _____

When the world seems to shine like you've had too much

wine, that's a - mor - é. _____ Bells will

ring, ting - a - ling - a - ling, ting - a - ling - a - ling, and you'll sing, "Vee - ta

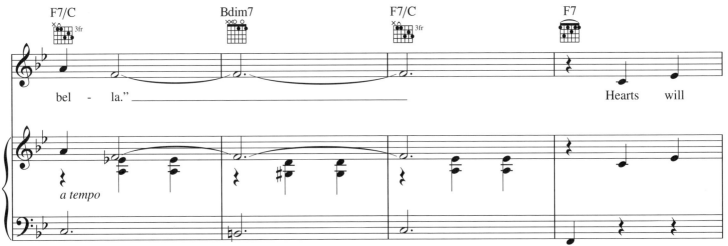

bel - la." _____ Hearts will

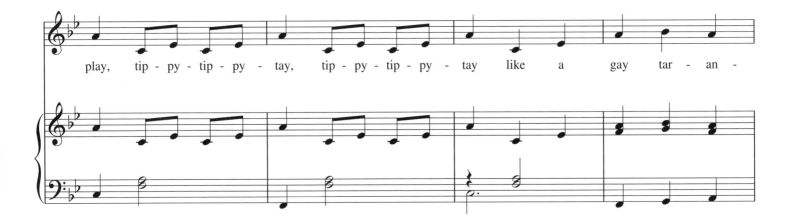

play, tip - py - tip - py - tay, tip - py - tip - py - tay like a gay tar - an -

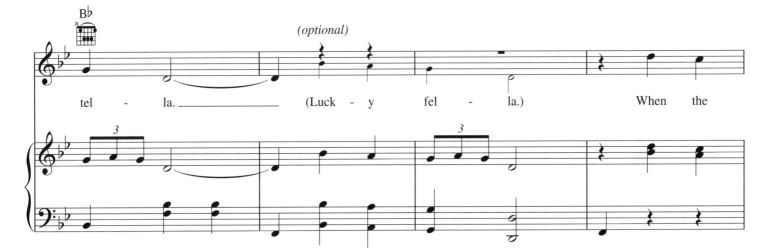

tel - la. _____ (Luck - y fel - la.) When the

stars make you drool just like pas - ta fa - zool, that's a -

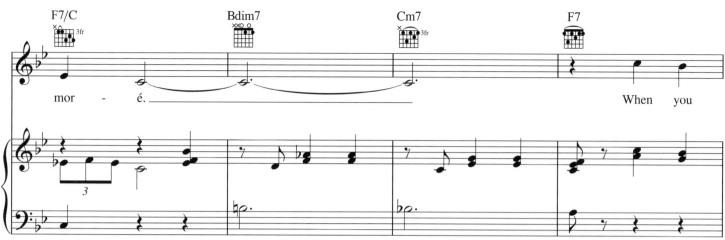

mor - é. _____ When you

dance down the street with a cloud at your feet, you're in

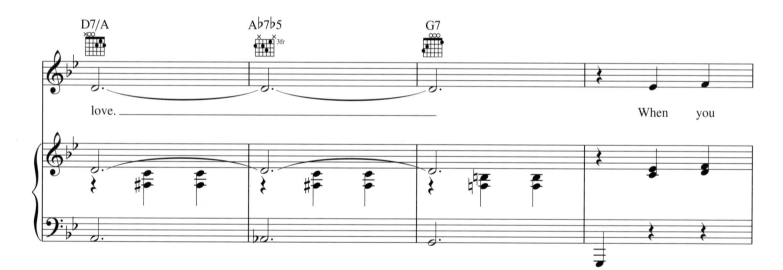

love. _____ When you

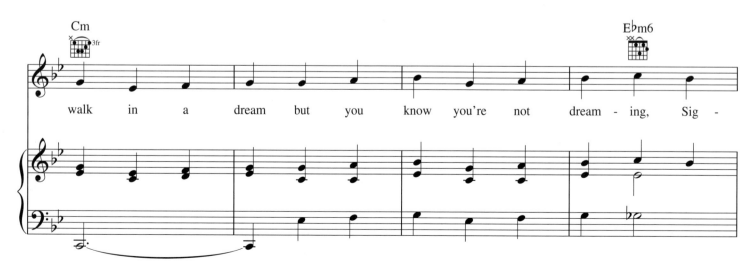

walk in a dream but you know you're not dream-ing, Sig -

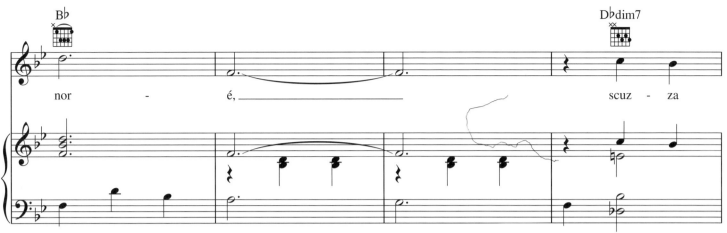

nor - é, _____ scuz - za

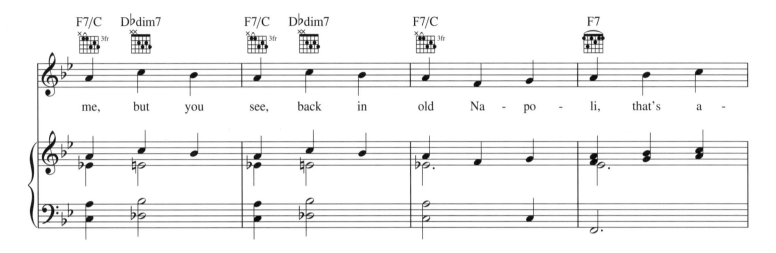

me, but you see, back in old Na - po - li, that's a -

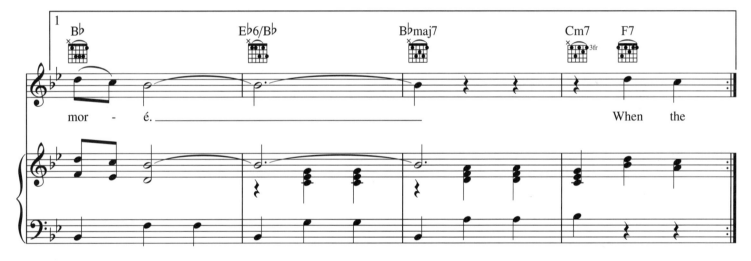

mor - é. _____ When the

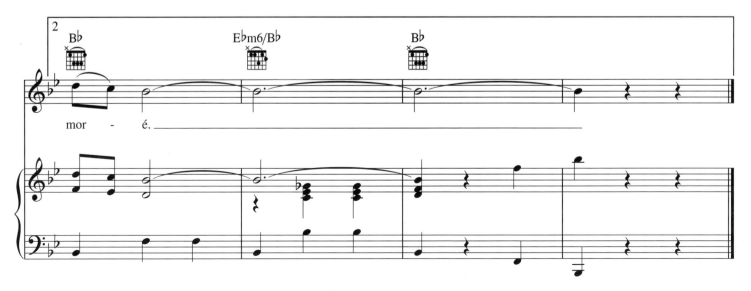

mor - é. _____

THREE COINS IN THE FOUNTAIN

from THREE COINS IN THE FOUNTAIN

Words by SAMMY CAHN
Music by JULE STYNE

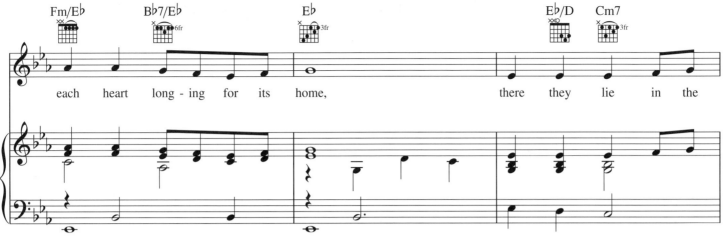

each heart long-ing for its home, there they lie in the

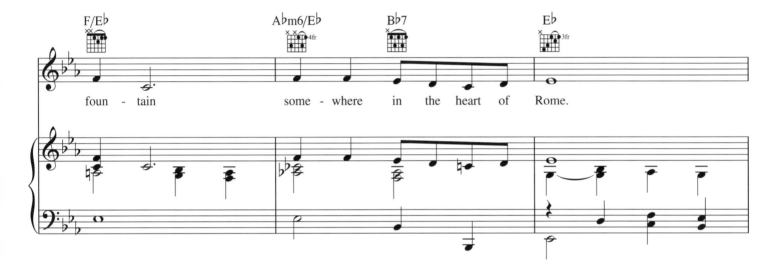

foun-tain some-where in the heart of Rome.

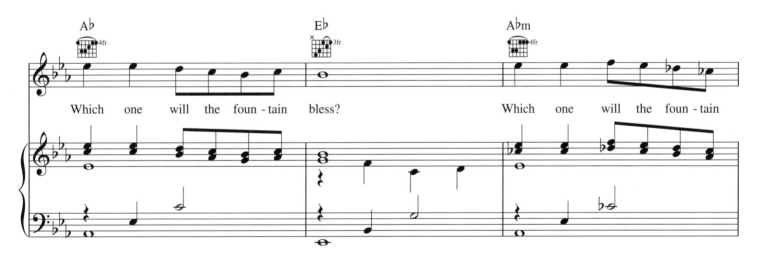

Which one will the foun-tain bless? Which one will the foun-tain

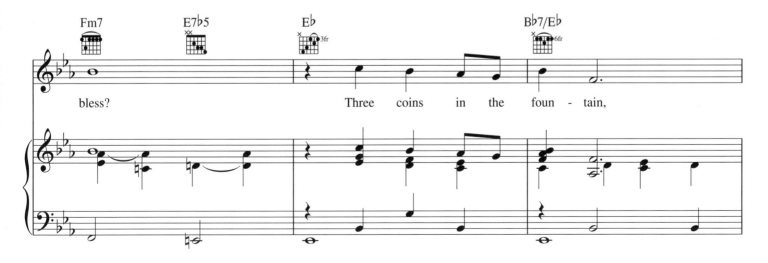

bless? Three coins in the foun-tain,

TILL WE TWO ARE ONE

Words by TOM GLAZER
Music by LARRY and BILLY MARTIN

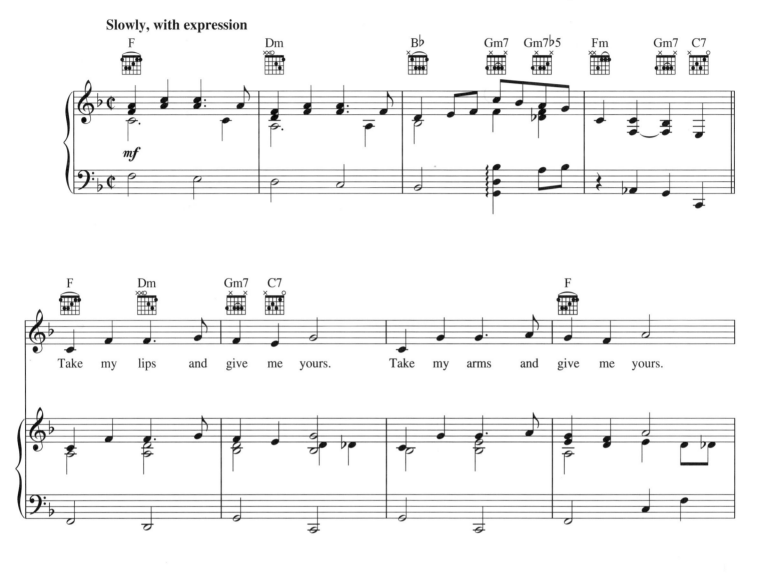

Just one kiss, if we should dare. Just one love for

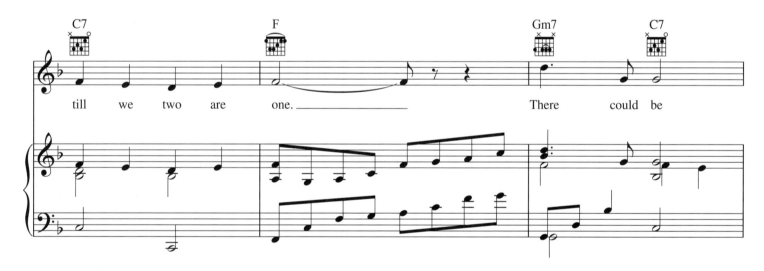

us to share. Just one ec - sta - sy is there,

till we two are one. _____ There could be

heav - en - ly dreams we take and give for;

thrill - ing - ly, will - ing - ly, mo - ments that we

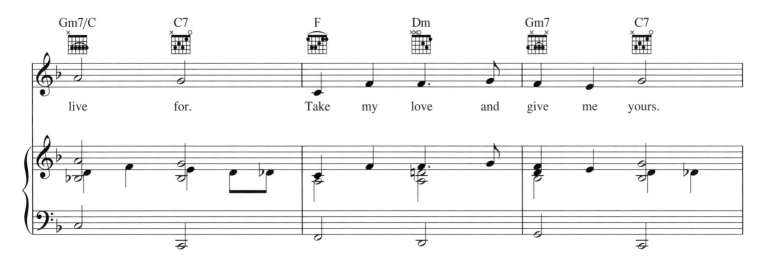

live for. Take my love and give me yours.

Take my life and give me yours. Take my soul and

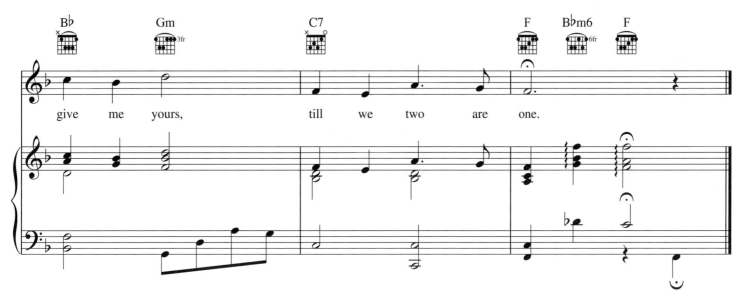

give me yours, till we two are one.

TRUE LOVE
from HIGH SOCIETY

Words and Music by
COLE PORTER

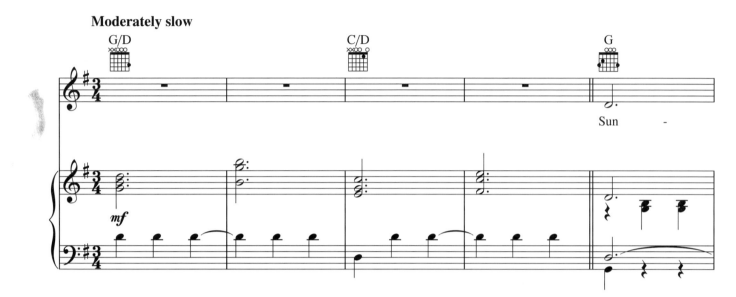

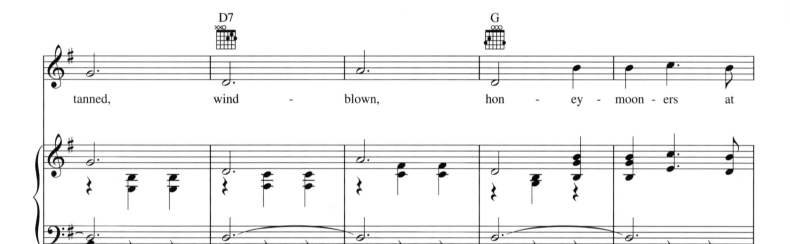

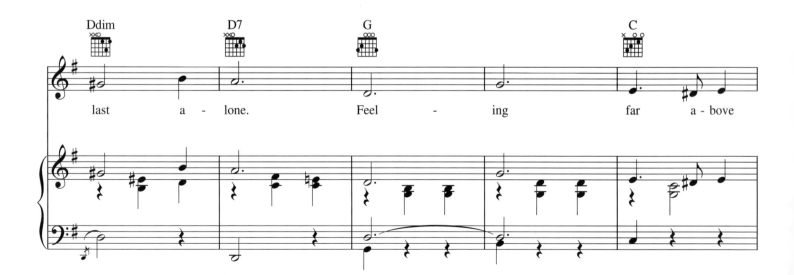

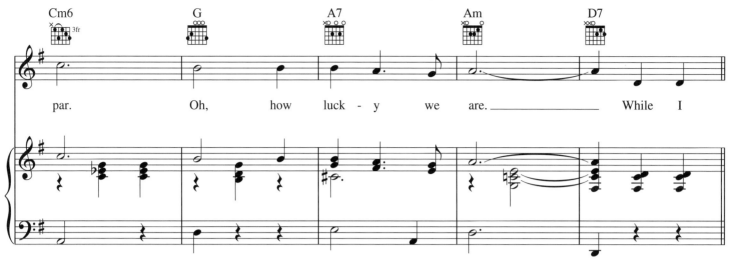

par. Oh, how luck-y we are._____ While I

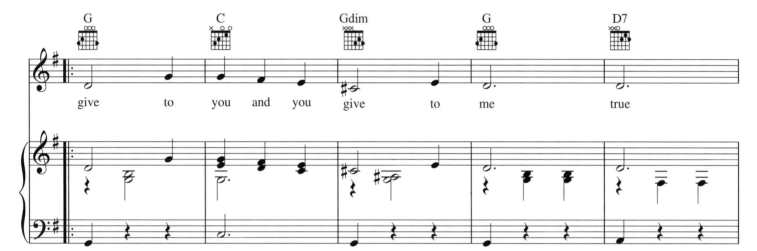

give to you and you give to me true

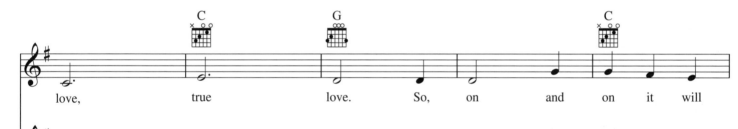

love, true love. So, on and on it will

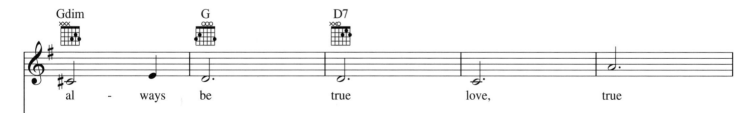

al - ways be true love, true

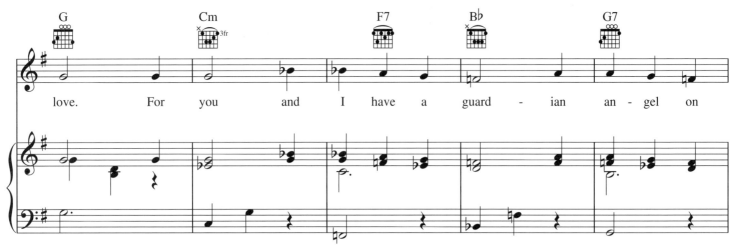

love. For you and I have a guard - ian an - gel on

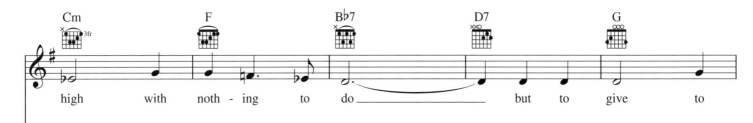

high with noth - ing to do _____ but to give to

you and to give to me love for - ev - er

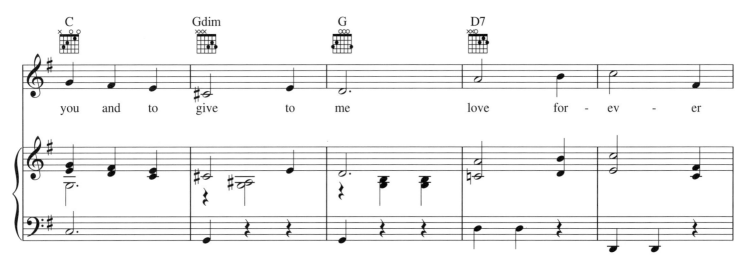

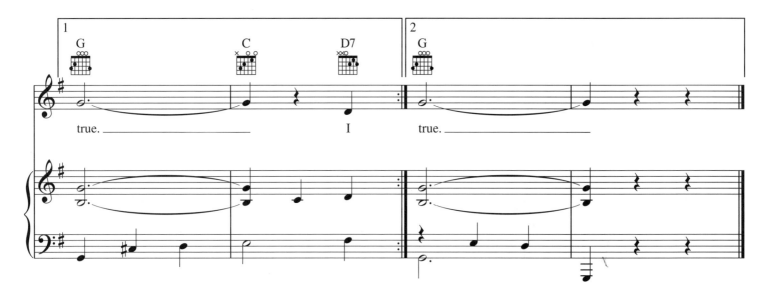

1
true. _____ I

2
true. _____

UNCHAINED MELODY
from the Motion Picture UNCHAINED

Lyric by HY ZARET
Music by ALEX NORTH

Whoa, _____ my _____ love, _____ my

dar - lin', _____ I've hun - gered for _____ your _

_____ touch a long, lone - ly

UNFORGETTABLE

Words and Music by
IRVING GORDON

WHEN I FALL IN LOVE

from ONE MINUTE TO ZERO

Words by EDWARD HEYMAN
Music by VICTOR YOUNG

Slowly, with much feeling

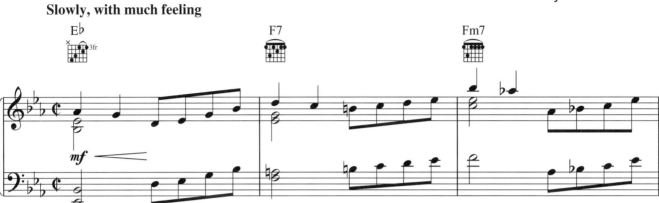

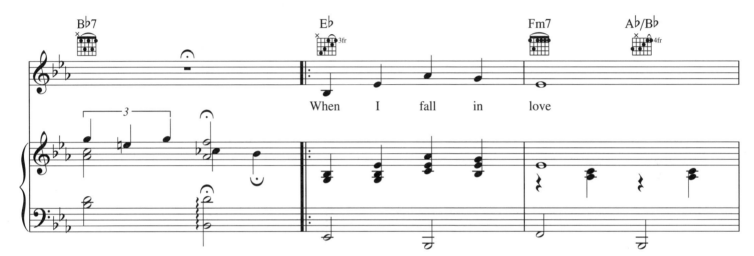

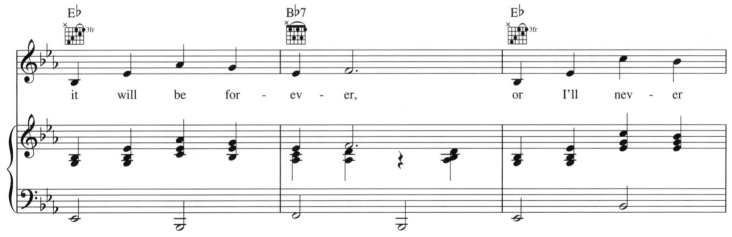

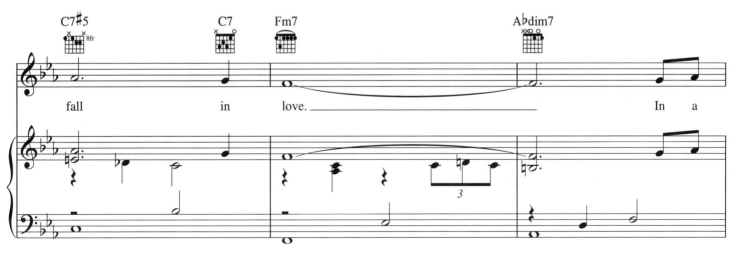

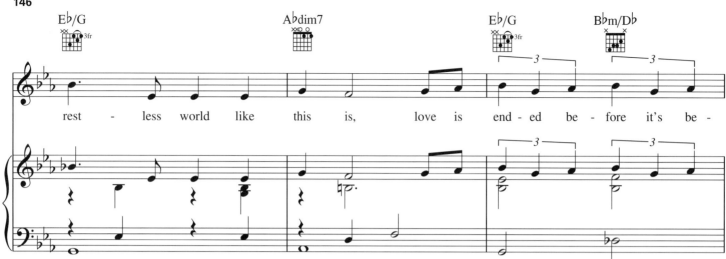

rest - less world like this is, love is end - ed be - fore it's be -

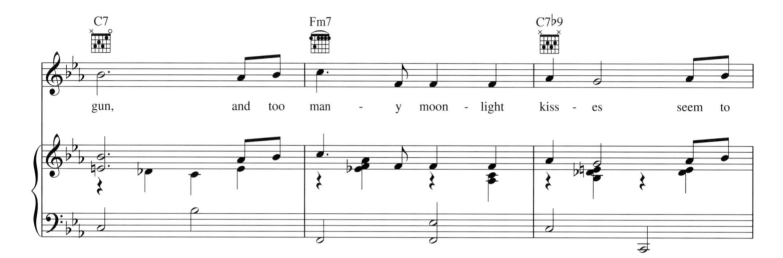

gun, and too man - y moon - light kiss - es seem to

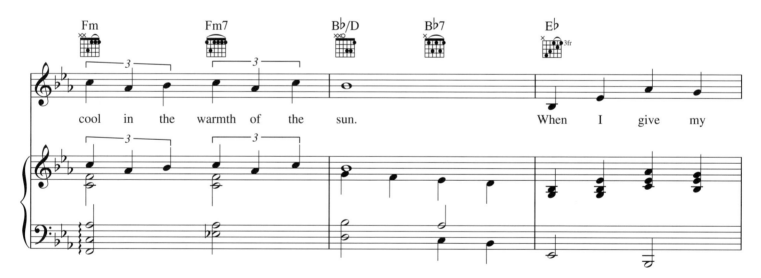

cool in the warmth of the sun. When I give my

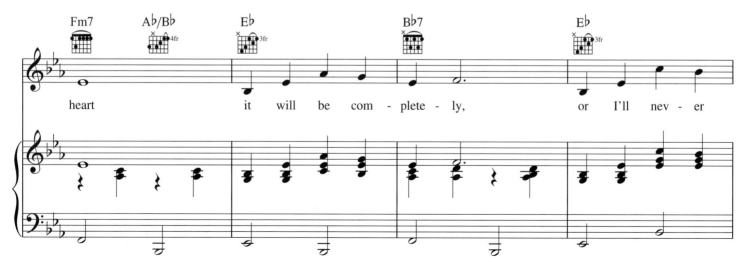

heart it will be com - plete - ly, or I'll nev - er

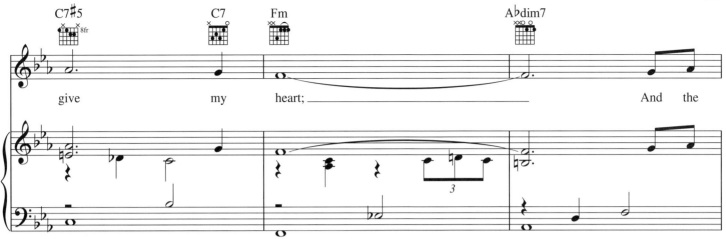

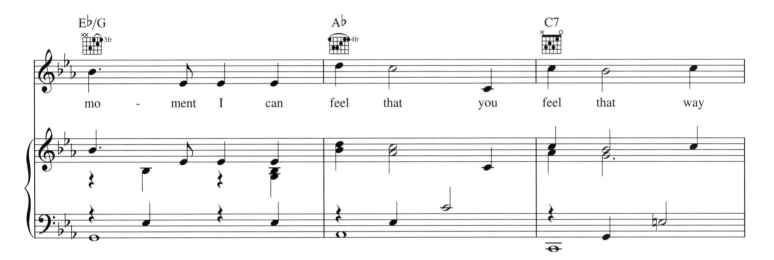

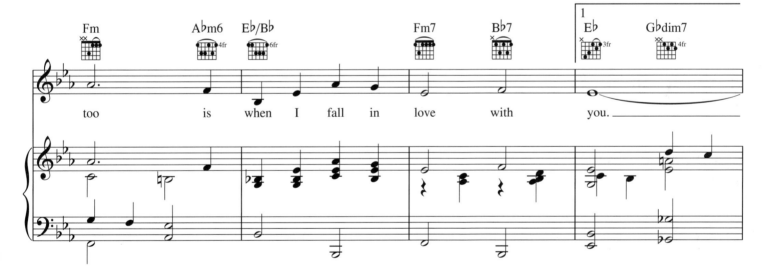

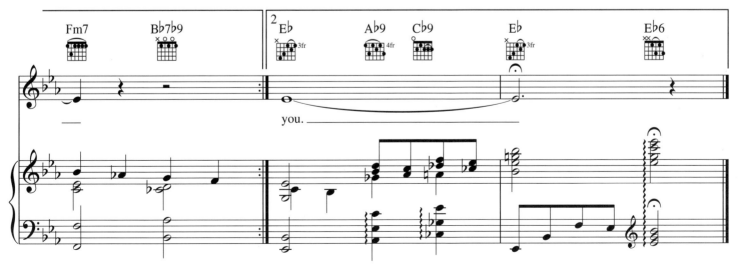

WHY

Words and Music by BOB MARCUCCI
and PETER DeANGELIS

oth - er. _____ And with our faith and

trust, there could be no oth - er. Why, 'cause I love you,

why, 'cause you love me. I _____ think you're aw - f'ly sweet, why, be - cause I

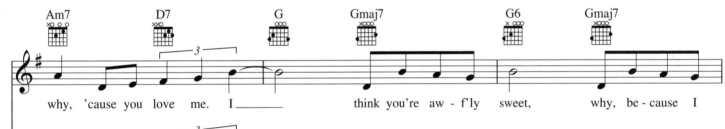

love you. _____ You say I'm your spe - cial

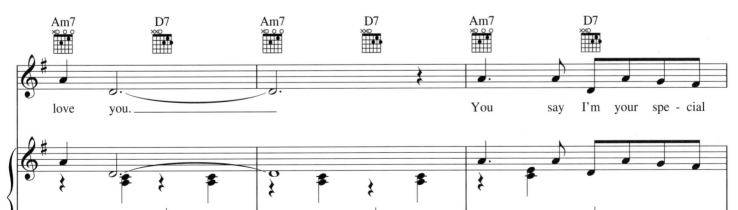

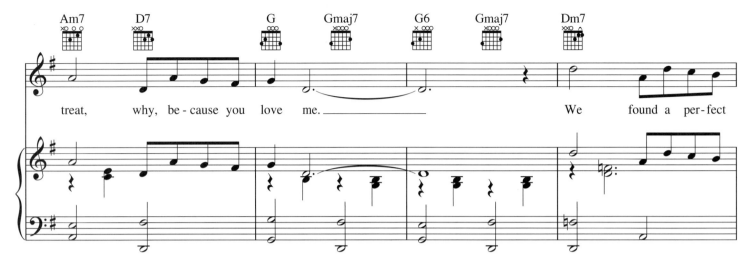

treat, why, be-cause you love me. _____ We found a per-fect

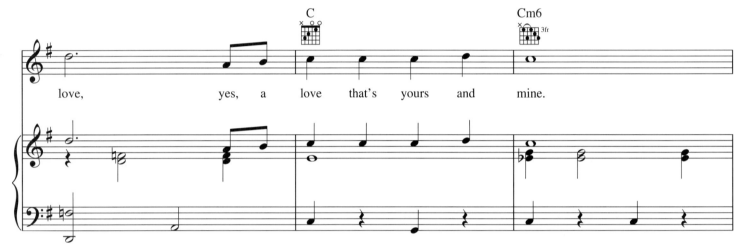

love, yes, a love that's yours and mine.

I love you and you love me all the time.

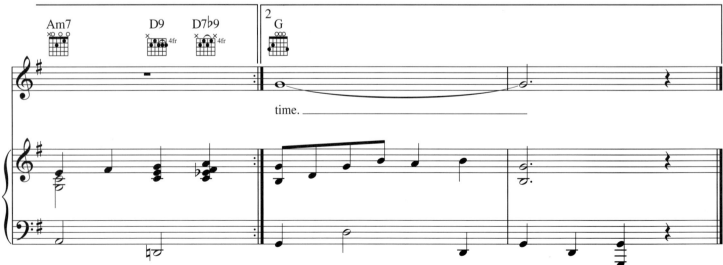

time. _____

YOUNG AT HEART

from YOUNG AT HEART

Words by CAROLYN LEIGH
Music by JOHNNY RICHARDS

THE WONDER OF YOU

Words and Music by
BAKER KNIGHT

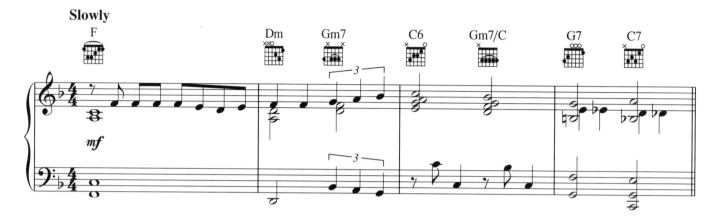

When no one else can un - der - stand me,
And when you smile, the world is bright - er.
You'll nev - er know how much I love you.

when ev - 'ry - thing I do is wrong,
You touch my hand and I'm a king.
My love is yours and yours a - lone,

you give me love and con - so -
Your kiss to me is worth a
and it's so won - der - ful to

la - tion.
for - tune.
have you,

You give me hope to car - ry on,
Your love to me is ev - 'ry - thing,
to have you for my ver - y own.

and you
and you're
Guess I'll

try to show your love for me in ev - 'ry - thing you
al - ways there to lend a hand in all I try to
nev - er know the rea - son why you love me as you

do.
do.
do.

That's the won - der,

the won - der of

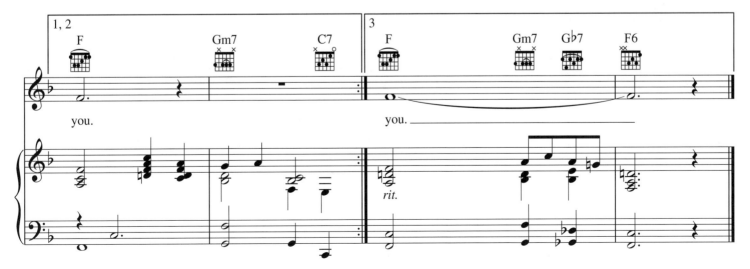

you.

you.

YOU ARE BEAUTIFUL

from FLOWER DRUM SONG

Lyrics by OSCAR HAMMERSTEIN II
Music by RICHARD RODGERS

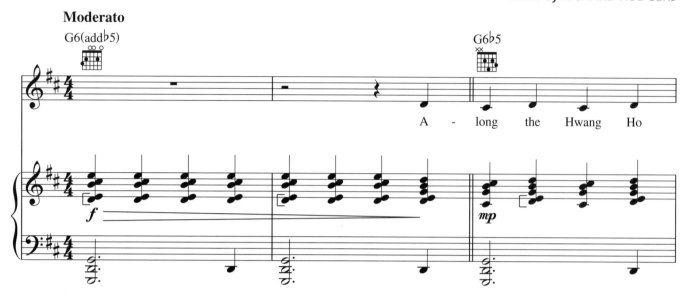

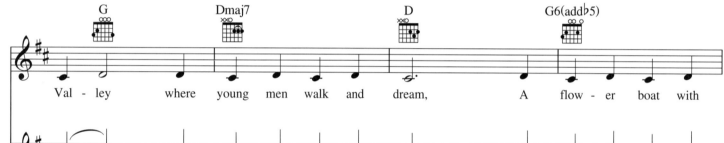

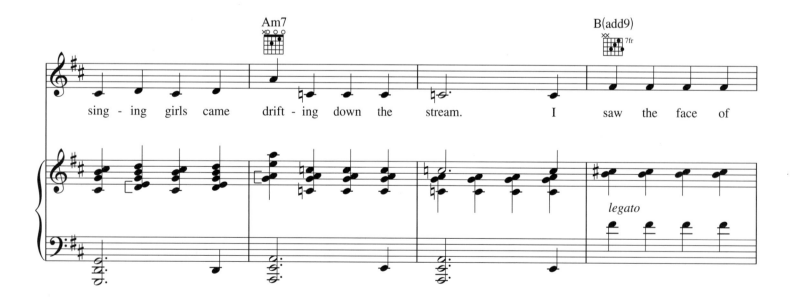

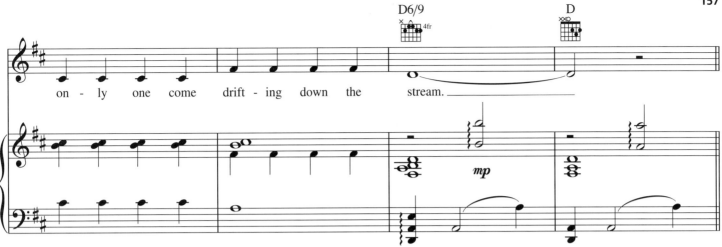

on - ly one come drift - ing down the stream.

Refrain (*tranquillo*)

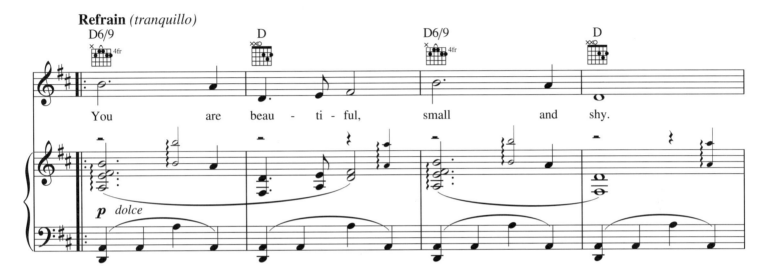

You are beau - ti - ful, small and shy.

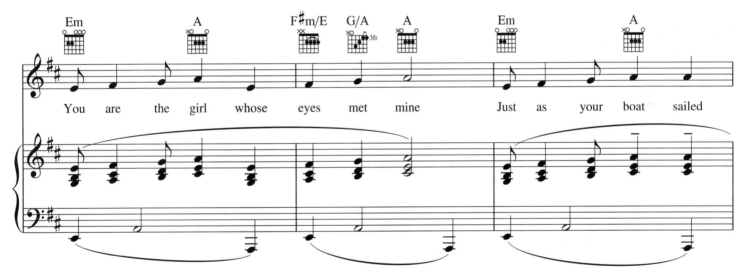

You are the girl whose eyes met mine Just as your boat sailed

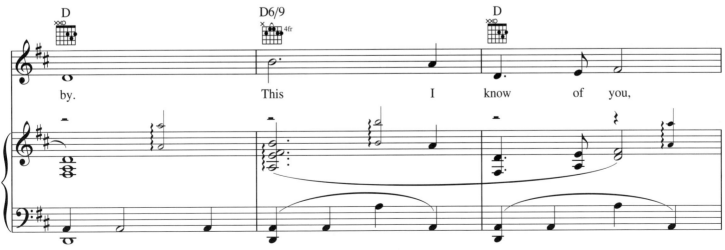

by. This I know of you,

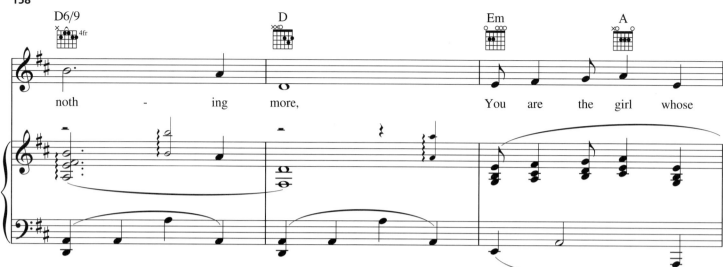

noth - ing more, You are the girl whose

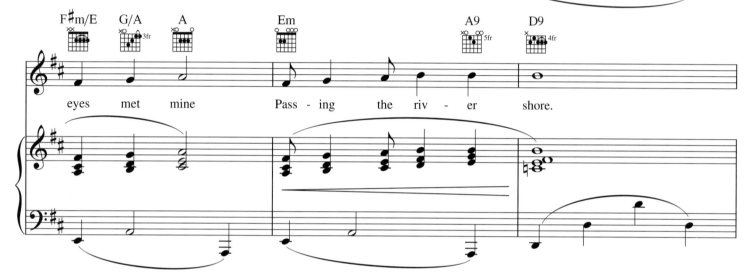

eyes met mine Pass - ing the riv - er shore.

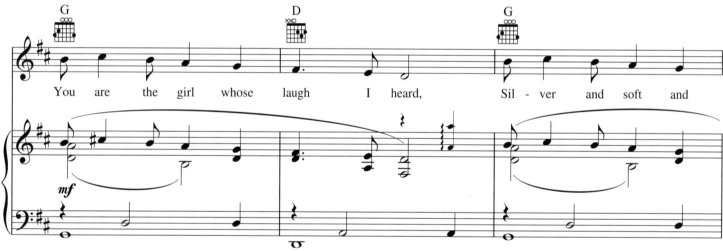

You are the girl whose laugh I heard, Sil - ver and soft and

bright; Soft as the fall of lo - tus leaves

YOU BELONG TO ME

Words and Music by PEE WEE KING,
REDD STEWART and CHILTON PRICE

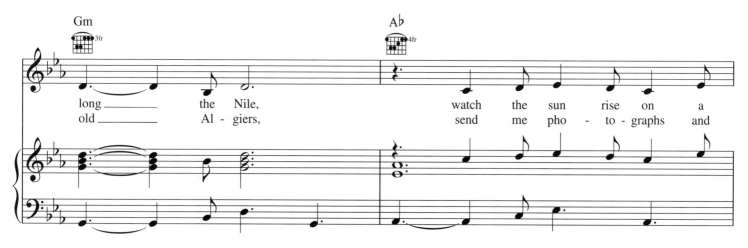

See the pyr - a - mids a -
See the mar - ket - place in

long _____ the Nile,
old _____ Al - giers,

watch the sun rise on a
send me pho - to - graphs and

trop - ic isle,
sou - ve - nirs,

just re - mem - ber, dar - ling,
just re - mem - ber when a

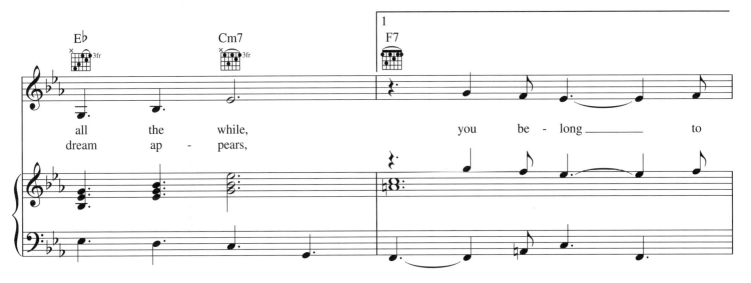

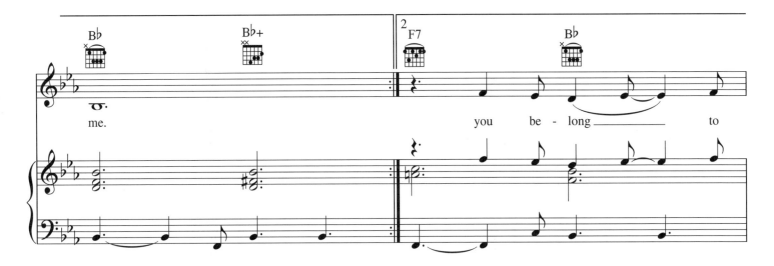

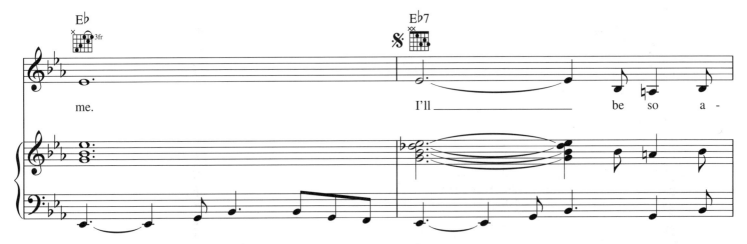

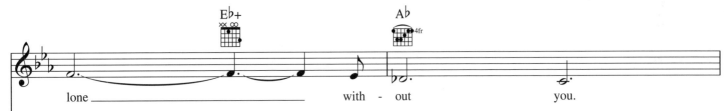

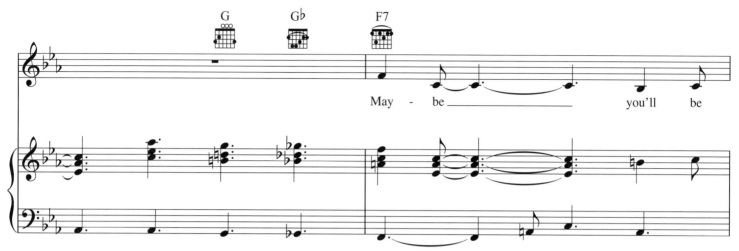

May - be _____ you'll be

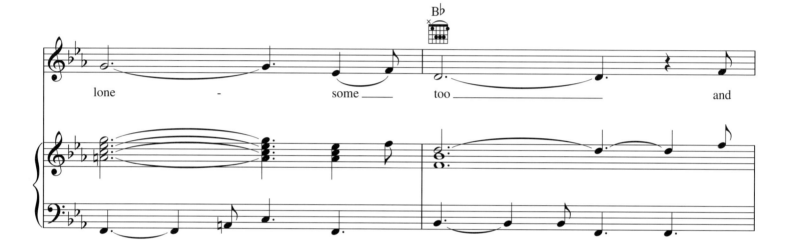

lone - some ____ too _____ and

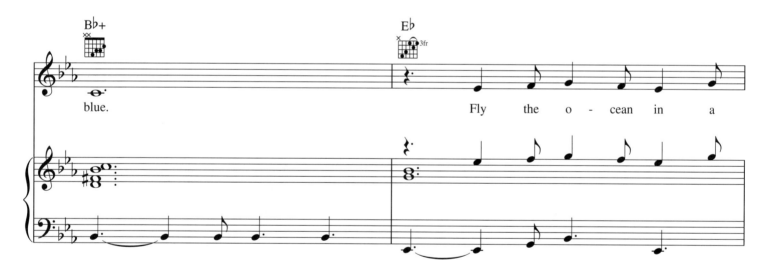

blue. Fly the o - cean in a

sil - ver plane, see the jun - gle when it's

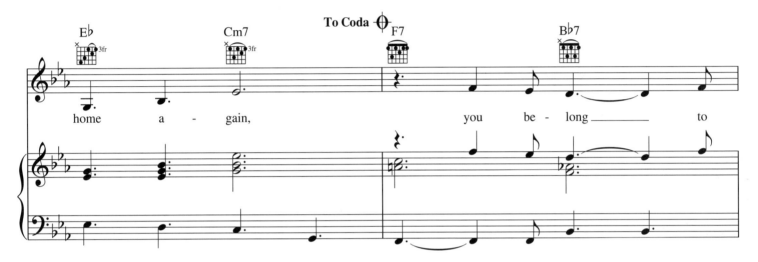

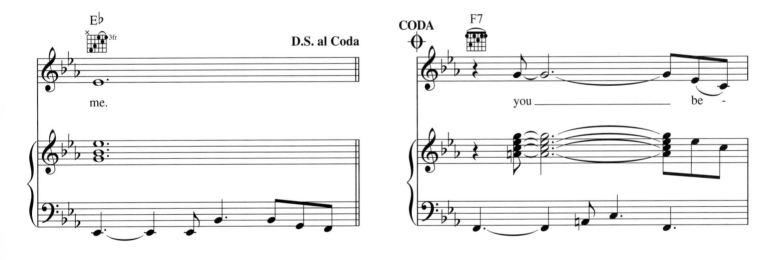

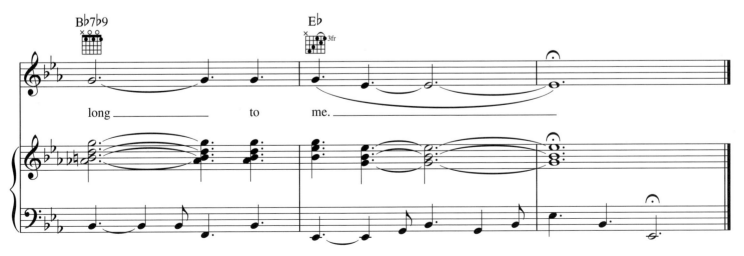

(I Wonder Why?)
YOU'RE JUST IN LOVE
from the Stage Production CALL ME MADAM

Words and Music by
IRVING BERLIN

I hear sing - ing and there's no one there. ___

I smell blos - soms and the trees are bare. ___

All day long I seem to walk on air, ___ I won - der

why? _____ I won - der why? _____

I keep toss - ing in my sleep at night. _____

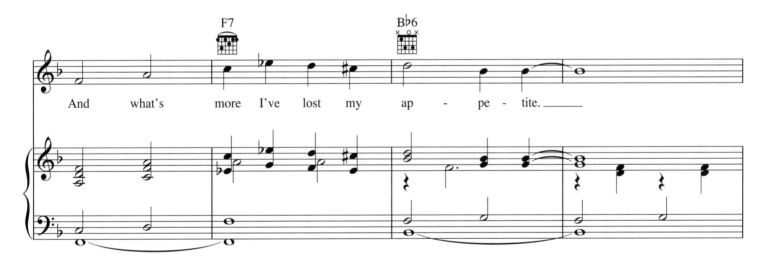

And what's more I've lost my ap - pe - tite. _____

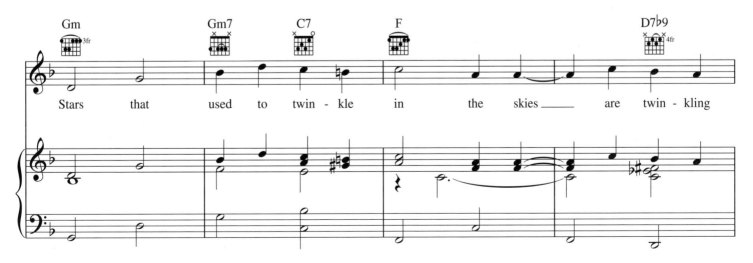

Stars that used to twin - kle in the skies _____ are twin - kling

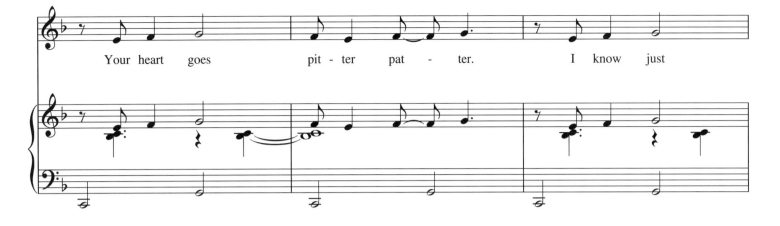

Your heart goes pit - ter pat - - ter. I know just

what's the mat - ter, be - cause I've been there once __ or twice. __

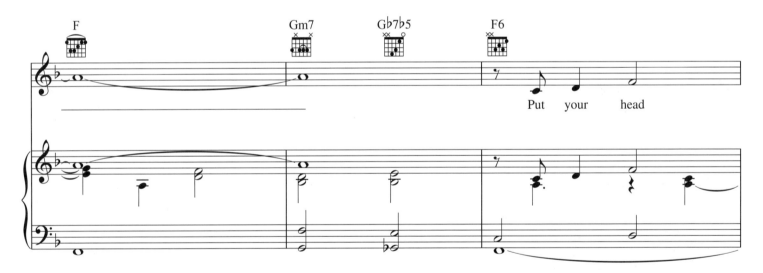

F   Gm7   Gb7b5   F6

Put your head

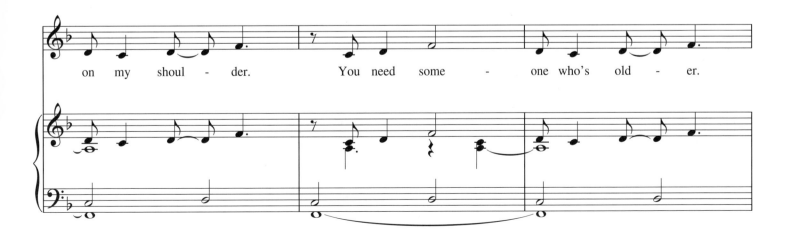

on my shoul - der. You need some - one who's old - er.

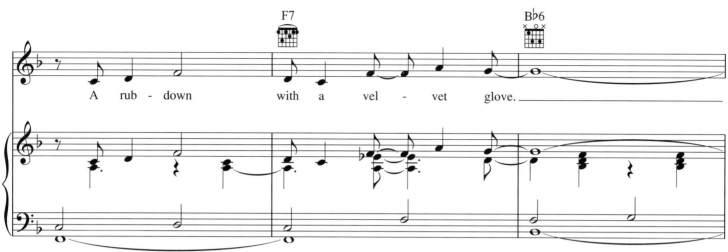

A rub - down with a vel - vet glove. ____

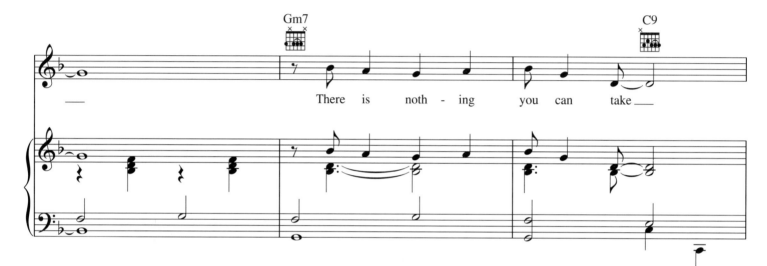

____ There is noth - ing you can take ___

to re - lieve that pleas - ant ache. ___ You're not sick, you're

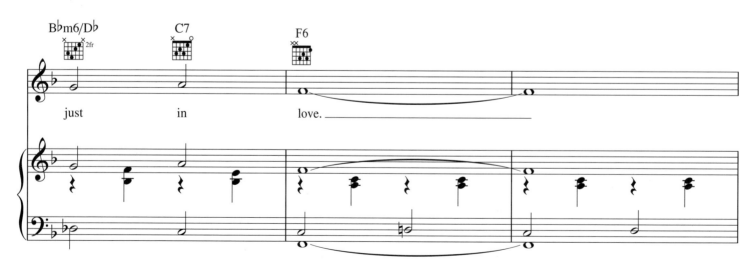

just in love. ____

I hear sing-ing and there's no one there. __

You don't need an-a-lyz-ing, it is not

__ I smell blos-soms and the

so sur-pris-ing that you feel ver-y strange __ but nice.

trees are bare. __ All day long I seem to

Your heart goes pit-ter pat-ter.

YOUNG LOVE

Words and Music by
RIC CARTEY

ev - er ____ in my heart. ____

love ____ for you ____ or for me. ____ Young

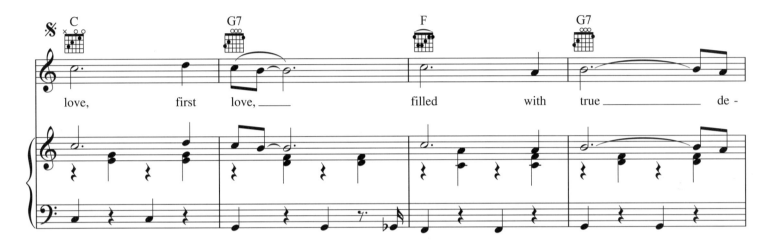

love, first love, ____ filled with true ____ de-

vo - tion. ____ Young love, our love ____ we share with

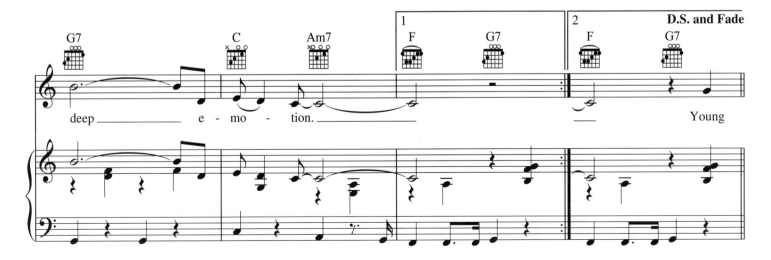

deep ____ e - mo - tion. ____ Young